WHAT YOUR COLLEAGUES ARE SAYING . . .

Anderson authentically engages with parents unlike any educational leader we have known. She details her time-tested recipe for success to empower other educators to do this work. If you're ready to stop tinkering with parent engagement and want to build collaborations that transform the lives of your students and families, you must read this book.

—**William Parrett and Kathleen Budge**
Authors, *Turning High-Poverty Schools into High-Performing Schools* (ASCD, 2020) and *Disrupting Poverty: Five Powerful Classroom Practices* (ASCD, 2018)
Director Emeritus, Center for School Improvement, Boise State University
Professor Emerita, College of Education, Boise State University
Sebring, Florida

Many parents want to be, and should be, actively included in the universal village that raises their child. Anderson's vast set of experiences and impressive body of expertise provide an authentic, faithful road map to that end.

—**Beryl Ann New**
Retired, Director of Certified Personnel and Equity, Topeka Public Schools
Region 2 Commissioner, Kansas African American Affairs Commission
Topeka, Kansas

Anderson provides a powerful book, painting a picture rich with illustrations as to the importance of engaging families. Each chapter includes lived and learned experiences that will leave footprints as you envision integrated tiered systems of support with families at the forefront.

—**Kathleen Lynne Lane**
Distinguished Professor and Associate Vice Chancellor for Research
University of Kansas
Lawrence, Kansas

I am grateful to leaders like Anderson, who leverages strategies to improve the overall well-being of children and their families in the school districts she leads.

—**Constance Gully**
President and Chief Executive Officer
Parents as Teachers National Center
St. Louis, Missouri

Anderson's book is a testament to her transformational leadership. It serves as an inspirational resource for communities seeking to build stronger connections between schools and families, utilizing a public health approach to guide groundbreaking change.

—**Cristi Cain**
Director, Local Public Health Program
Kansas Department of Health and Environment
Topeka, Kansas

This book is a testament to Anderson's passion for empowering parents to become active partners in their children's education. Through practical strategies and personal anecdotes, she illustrates how to equip parents to engage meaningfully in their child's learning journey.

—**Michelle Hubbard**
2023 Kansas Superintendent of the Year Superintendent
Shawnee Mission School District
Shawnee, Kansas

Anderson provides lived experience and truly has walked the talk. Her writing exemplifies the profound understanding that meeting students and families where they are, without judgment, while maintaining an open mind is paramount. Her dedication to connecting with families and fostering community ties underscores her deep-seated passion and compassion for those she serves. It's truly remarkable writing.

—**Ashley Goss**
Deputy Secretary for Public Health
Kansas Department of Health and Environment
Topeka, Kansas

Building Parent Capacity in High-Poverty Schools

In loving memory of Dr. Stanley Anderson, my incredible husband and a tremendous father to our two children, Whitney and Christopher, who inspire me daily to serve ALL children as if they are my own.

Building Parent Capacity in High-Poverty Schools

Actions for Authentic Impact

Tiffany C. Anderson

CORWIN
A Sage Company

FOR INFORMATION:

Corwin

A SAGE Company

2455 Teller Road

Thousand Oaks, California 91320

(800) 233-9936

www.corwin.com

SAGE Publications Ltd.

1 Oliver's Yard

55 City Road

London EC1Y 1SP

United Kingdom

SAGE Publications India Pvt. Ltd.

Unit No 323-333, Third Floor, F-Block

International Trade Tower Nehru Place

New Delhi 110 019

India

SAGE Publications Asia-Pacific Pte. Ltd.

18 Cross Street #10-10/11/12

China Square Central

Singapore 048423

Vice President and Editorial
  Director: Monica Eckman

Senior Acquisitions Editor: Tanya Ghans

Content Development
  Manager: Desirée A. Bartlett

Senior Editorial Assistant: Nyle De Leon

Project Editor: Amy Schroller

Copy Editor: Heather Kerrigan

Typesetter: C&M Digitals (P) Ltd.

Proofreader: Dennis Webb

Indexer: Integra

Cover Designer: Janet Kiesel

Marketing Manager: Melissa Duclos

Printed in the United States of America

ISBN 978-1-0719-4623-7

Library of Congress Control Number: 2024935128

This book is printed on acid-free paper.

24 25 26 27 28 10 9 8 7 6 5 4 3 2 1

Contents

Foreword

In this strikingly practical book, Tiffany C. Anderson explains what every teacher and school leader knows—we cannot do in six hours a day what families and community members are not doing the other 18 hours of the day. With a compelling sense of urgency, Dr. Anderson calls on all of us in education to recognize the imperative to build parent capacity. After years in which the communication between families and the school was largely ignored, the author encourages us to establish genuine relationships.

There are four essential transformations that educators, leaders, policymakers, and parents should embrace: (1) work with parents as partners, (2) prioritize clarity in all communications, (3) focus on real and practical solutions, and (4) budget for success. First, we must change from announcing policies to parents to genuine understanding of their needs and working with them as partners. I do not believe that any teacher or school leader intentionally alienates parents, but too often we alienate families with our archaic and punitive systems of feedback. When students and parents feel threatened, they are reluctant to collaborate with schools. The second transformation is from jargon to clarity. While educational professionals may understand precisely what "phonological awareness" or "critical thinking" means, not all parents are fluent in education-speak, especially parents for whom English is not their first language. On student report cards and curriculum documents, we must focus on clarity and, as Dr. Anderson encourages us, seek first to understand others before we ask them to understand us.

Third, we must move from rhetoric to reality. With powerful examples from her life as a leader, Dr. Anderson takes the building of parent capacity out of the shadows to very practical application. Particularly helpful are her questions for reflection that can be the subject of joint meetings with school staff members and parents. Fourth, we must move from bake sales to "BUDGET," the acronym Dr. Anderson uses to explain the relationship between funding and meeting the needs of students and parents. While schools and communities always seem to find the funding to support students after they fail, the author makes the case that prevention offers the greatest return on investment.

It is especially noteworthy that Dr. Anderson leads the educational system that was at the center of the *Brown v. Board of Education of Topeka* case in the 1950's. Seventy years later the nation continues to struggle with the impact of inequities on student achievement and life-long success. These challenges must be met not merely by schools, but with a community-wide alliance that includes the voices of parents, students, teachers, leaders, and policymakers. I have watched as Dr. Anderson extends her impact from pre-kindergarten children to centenarians, who bring a sense of history, equity, and justice to future generations.

This is a book to be studied and discussed. If it provokes some debate, that is great, because as Dr. Anderson knows better than most people, respectful divergent thinking is the rocket fuel of thoughtful discussions and community building. The educational world is fortunate to learn from her insight, experience, and passion.

Douglas Reeves
Author of *Fearless Schools*
Boston, Massachusetts

Acknowledgments

I thank God for leading me in this project. I am forever grateful for the fearless parents who were the plaintiffs in the landmark *Brown v. Board of Education* case in 1954 that opened the door for me to become the first Black woman superintendent in Topeka, Kansas.

A special thank you is extended to my family, which includes my parents, Rev. Larry Brown and Dr. Edna Montgomery, who taught me how to serve as a wife, a parent advocate, and an educator; to my late husband, Dr. Stanley Anderson; and my two children, Whitney and Christopher, whose tremendous capacity to love and serve others inspires me daily.

This book would not be possible without the Corwin staff that include, but are not limited to, Tanya Ghans, Sara Johnson, the editing and publishing staff, and the researchers, authors, and educational thought partners who I continue to learn from in education.

Serving in education is a privilege and a ministry of love. Thank you to the Methodist church I am a member of, Church of the Resurrection, and the many other churches and organizations for partnering with educators to care for and serve the whole family. I sincerely thank the many past and present educators, school boards, and school-district communities that I have had the privilege to serve alongside.

PUBLISHER'S ACKNOWLEDGMENTS

Corwin gratefully acknowledges the contributions of the following reviewers:

Tanna Nicely, Principal
South Knoxville Elementary School
Blaine, Tennessee

Debra Paradowski, Associate Principal
Arrowhead Union High School
Hartland, Wisconsin

About the Author

After serving as a teacher, principal, assistant superintendent, and superintendent, in 2016 **Tiffany C. Anderson, EdD,** became the first Black woman superintendent for Topeka Public Schools in Topeka, Kansas, home of *Brown v. Board of Education*, the Supreme Court case that ended legal segregation. Dr. Anderson has served as a school administrator for twenty-six years and under her leadership, Topeka has earned multiple local, state, and national awards, including three Magna Awards from the National School Boards Association for innovative approaches impacting families and the community. Additionally, she has served alongside educators and parents leading three districts in gaining full accreditation in Virginia, Missouri, and Kansas. Over her twenty years serving as a superintendent, Dr. Anderson's transformational leadership approach in addressing the needs of families in the community has been captured in articles, speaking engagements, a docuseries, and, in 2016, she was selected by *EdWeek* as one of the nation's sixteen Leaders to Learn From. In 2023, the American Association of School Administrators recognized Dr. Anderson with the national 2023 Women in School Leadership Award. Dr. Anderson attended Saint Louis University for her bachelor's degree, University of Missouri St. Louis for her master's, and Saint Louis University for her doctorate. In 2022, Dr. Anderson attended St. Paul School of Theology and Nazarene Theological Seminary where she received her master's in divinity. She is a professor of practice for Kansas State University, and she has served as adjunct faculty for multiple universities and for the Association for Supervision and Curriculum Development. Dr. Anderson is a public health advocate, and over the past decade she has championed initiatives in public schools and post-secondary settings on behalf of educators and families in Kansas as a parent, school superintendent, and board member on the Kansas Board of Regents for the Technical Education Authority.

Introduction

"The capacity to learn is a gift, the ability to learn is a skill, and the willingness to learn is a choice."

—Herbert (2000)

We have tremendous capacity to develop, learn, and grow. Through research and experience, I have witnessed the power to engage the collective school community with parents as a key lever to transformational change.

I am also a product of parents whose capacity was built through the school system over time, so I have a deeply rooted passion for this work. By sharing with you a little about my story, you can see the power that comes from building parent capacity.

I was raised by two educators who grew up and were in school during the 1940s and 1950s, the years in which *Brown v. Board of Education* occurred. Following the court decision, my mother and her sister became two of the first Black women to integrate Soldan High School in St. Louis, Missouri. My mother's parents, Edna and Obia Montgomery, wanted my mother and her sister to have equal access and opportunities to the educational resources their white neighbors had access to in the city of St. Louis. Their advocacy for their children and their willingness to remain engaged with public schools changed the future of my mother's life and later mine.

My father, who was raised by his aunt and uncle during that same period, had a very different experience. While he had the loving, strict upbringing of extended family, they lived in a segregated part of St. Louis. His aunt was a teacher in the city in all-Black schools, which led him to remain in all-Black schools through his high school graduation, near his home in St. Louis. He and his extended family were deeply involved in the all-Black schools and community, which shaped the spirit of advocacy and service of my father.

As a married couple, my parents participated in the Civil Rights Movement, and they ultimately moved into an integrated neighborhood in the suburbs of St. Louis County, Missouri, where they enrolled me in an elementary school that ensured I learned alongside students of diverse ethnic and racial backgrounds.

My parents participated in parent organizations in formal and informal ways. My mother volunteered as often as she could, both of my parents participated in the PTO/PTA organizations, they encouraged other parents to get involved, and they used every opportunity they could find to serve as a room parent and to meet with teachers. My mother even taught for the school system they placed me in for my elementary education. Through their involvement, I learned how the power of collective impact from parents in one neighborhood could make a difference. I was afforded every opportunity I could have dreamed of in public and private school because of my parent's capacity to engage and organize with other parents as advocates for the success of all children.

Just as my mother was one of the first Black students to integrate Soldan High School in the 1950s, my father later became one of the first Black stockbrokers at Merrill Lynch. Through their examples, I learned that you have to be willing to take the first steps so that others can take steps behind you. Without having a first, you will not have a second. If you do not open the door, it may stay closed forever. My parents paved the way for me to become the assistant superintendent and director of desegregation in one of the largest and highest performing districts in St. Louis County, the first Black and first woman superintendent in Montgomery County (Blacksburg, Virginia), and the first Black woman superintendent of Topeka Public Schools in Kansas. Parents have the power to change a generation, and that generation has the power to change the next generation. This is how we change the educational system into a system of hope, opportunity, and prosperity.

When parents engage to create experiences (in some cases, first experiences) for students, or to be the first to volunteer to partner and develop new systems and build them into ones that truly work, it creates sustainable school and neighborhood communities engineered by those who live in the community. Witnessing my parents in their efforts to galvanize communities as educators, and later as local pastors, set the example for me to build bridges with parents and schools in communities as the key lever to making schools work well for children. When parents have a strong capacity as the blueprint from which to build outcomes, their children have a solid framework and foundation to be the architects of their own destiny, crafting a future of hope for the generations that follow. Parental engagement today changes the future of education for the students and parents of tomorrow. Building parent capacity is about something bigger than us. It is about building a future of hope.

ABOUT THIS BOOK

This book brings together research and lived experiences to share practical tools, methods, and ideas that school leaders and educators can use to engage parents and build their capacity. The Lived and Learned sections feature stories from the various school districts in which I have worked or from other schools around the country doing great things in support of families and students. Each chapter also has an In Action section to show what it looks like when an element of this work is applied in different contexts. And each chapter ends with a Reflection and a full-page What?-So What?-Now What? section to help you apply the chapter ideas to your own contexts.

Chapter 1 defines parent capacity and makes the case for the urgency of engaging families in schools and establishing schools as the center of the community.

Chapter 2 looks at the difference between involvement and engagement. The chapter also brings to light the importance of an asset-based mindset when working with parents and how to build their capacity in the various roles that parents often take within a school.

Chapter 3 focuses on authenticity and what it means to be a good leader. It shares practical ways that leaders can walk the talk and truly affect change by understanding parents' needs, removing barriers of engagement, and building efficacy.

Chapter 4 examines the role of community partnerships. We can't do this work alone, and partnerships are key to removing barriers and building parents' capacity.

Chapter 5 discusses the elephant in the room—funding. The chapter sheds light on school funding and shares ideas for using dollars wisely and creatively in order to accomplish your vision.

Schools have tremendous capacity to shape the future. However, in order to shape the future, the relationship and connections that create systems have to be built, reinforced, and supported. This resource serves as one tool for educators, parents, and community members to gain new strategies that inspire, educate, and train others to make the dreams of our parents and those who came before us a reality.

CHAPTER 1

Understanding Parent Capacity and Its Role in Student Success

"Change will not come if we wait for some other person or some other time. We are the ones we've been waiting for. We are the change that we seek."

—Obama (2008)

Let's think back to the early 1950s. The decision in *Plessy v. Ferguson*, about sixty years prior, had provided a constitutional basis for racial segregation. And although the Supreme Court's intention was to uphold the Fourteenth Amendment's commitment to "equal protection under the law" for all citizens, in reality the ruling led to the devastating "separate but equal" doctrine, which opened the door to the Jim Crow era, physically dividing Americans in almost every aspect of daily life—housing, shopping, transportation, access to health care and adequate municipals, and especially education, just to name a few.

Segregated schools for Black children were often overcrowded and the buildings were underfunded and not maintained or upheld to safety standards. Students did not have enough access to necessary learning supplies, such as desks or books. And the materials they did have were worn out, old, and outdated. Students typically had to walk long distances or take buses to school, often extending their school day by hours.

By 1951, parents of Black children across the country began to speak up, especially those in Topeka, Kansas. Among others, Lucinda Todd, Zelma Henderson, Sadie Emanuel, Lena Carper, and Rev. Oliver Brown were tired of their children being bused across town to segregated schools, instead of being able to attend their neighborhood schools closer to home. So, they attempted to enroll their children in neighborhood schools, but were denied admittance because those schools were only for white children.

None of those parents were lawyers or had experience filing court cases—Lucinda was a teacher, Zelma was a beautician, Oliver was a welder and minister—but through the support of the NAACP and Thurgood Marshall, they eventually brought their concerns to the Supreme Court (along with the court cases of five others) in the historic class action lawsuit, *Brown v. Board of Education*.

In 1954, the Supreme Court voted unanimously in favor of the parents. Chief Justice Earl Warren wrote the decision stating, in part, "Segregation in public education is a denial of the equal protection of the laws. To separate some children from others of similar age and qualifications solely because of their race generates a feeling of inferiority as to their status in the community that may affect their hearts and minds in a way unlikely ever to be undone." The ruling held, "We conclude that in the field of public education the doctrine of 'separate but equal' has no place. Separate educational facilities are inherently unequal; segregation in public education is a denial of the equal protection of the laws."

This decision was a landmark victory. What those parents knew was that education is the great equalizer, and they were prepared to go to battle for their children to receive the education they deserved—and legally were entitled to—even if it seemed like David was taking on Goliath (1 Samuel 17). Through their case they demonstrated that resources matter, access to equal educational opportunities matter, and parent-educator partnerships matter. Ultimately, the *Brown v. Board* case was a catalyst for change through the Civil Rights Movement—barely one year later Rosa Parks refused to give up her seat to a white man on a bus in Montgomery, Alabama—and central to that movement were parents and community members advocating for equitable access to opportunities in order to end segregated practices and disrupt generational poverty.

> *Resources matter, access to educational opportunities matter, and parent-educator partnerships matter.*

Seventy years later, we are still working to realize the promise of *Brown v. Board of Education*. Although progress has been made since that court decision, we still see evidence of institutionalized racism, voter suppression, unfair housing opportunities, and inequitable educational practices. In 2023, the Supreme Court overturned affirmative action admission practices in higher education, effectively challenging a college or university's ability to ensure a racially diverse student population that reflects diverse perspectives, cultures, and backgrounds. Just as parents were key in 1954, they remain central to solutions in today's educational climate.

▶ Students and parents who initiated the landmark civil rights lawsuit *Brown v. Board of Education*, Topeka, Kansas, 1953. Front row from left, students Vicki Henderson, Donald Henderson, Linda Brown, James Emanuel, Nancy Todd, and Katherine Carper; back row from left, parents Zelma Henderson, Oliver Brown, Sadie Emanuel, Lucinda Todd, and Lena Carper. Photo by Carl Iwasaki/The LIFE Images Collection via Getty Images.

DEFINING PARENT CAPACITY

Parents are a child's first educator. The years in which a child's brain has the greatest growth are the first years from birth to when they enter school. They will be shaped by experiences with their parents or guardians. Therefore, just as we focus on building the capacity of our traditional school-level educators, we must also focus on building the capacity of the adults serving as parents to the current and future students of our schools so that when the children enter our schools for the first time and throughout their educational careers they are as prepared as possible for learning.

Pedro Noguera discusses the importance of context in many of his works, for example, *City Schools and the American Dream*, *Excellence Through Equity*, and *Creating the Opportunity to Learn*. He focuses on creating schools where a child's race or class is no longer a predictor of how well they might perform. I have found that in addition to school, context matters in our approach with parents, and it matters when addressing the conditions provided at home for students to learn. Noguera states, "Unless we believe that those who have more are inherently superior to those who have less, we should be troubled by the fact that patterns of achievement are often fairly predictable, particularly with respect to students' race and class" (Boykin & Noguera, 2011). Imagine if we could create communities in which race and class was not a predictor of performance. This is possible if we engage families and change the conditions in which they live. Simply put, the context in which a student lives matters. The ability of parents, or the individuals serving in the role of parents, to grow and develop in support of their child matters.

Let's look more closely at building capacity and what this means. Fullan (2012) writes, "capacity building is about encouraging and supporting teachers in their desire to be excellent at their craft. The end result of this work is that there is deeper motivation on the part of teachers to continue their growth unencumbered." Since we know that parents are children's first teachers, we can in essence replace the word *teachers* with the word *parents*. When we do that, capacity building then becomes about encouraging and supporting parents in their desire to be excellent at parenting. This is the focus of parent capacity: helping parents build their intrinsic desire to support their child's growth and learning.

Similarly, self-efficacy can be described as the confidence we have in ourselves, and collective efficacy as the confidence we have in our group to make a difference (DeWitt, 2019; Tschannen-Moran & Barr, 2004). There is a direct correlation to parents. When parents feel empowered to be the change, to help uplift, and problem solve needs in their schools as educational partners, they are empowered to engage more because their ability to have a greater impact has grown.

> *Parent capacity is the degree in which parents are empowered and intrinsically engaged to support student learning and growth.*

My definition of parent capacity is the degree in which parents are empowered and intrinsically engaged to support student learning and growth.

WHY PARENT CAPACITY MATTERS: THE URGENCY TO RESPOND

We all have the capacity to learn and grow. The amount in which we are willing to grow depends largely on our experience, our mindset, and preparation. In visiting schools across the country, school leaders often cite lack of parental involvement as a challenge area. The more time I spend discussing this challenge, the clearer it becomes that parent capacity is the root issue. Once capacity is developed in ongoing ways, parents and the school can do more as partners in education. Without parents, schools are limited because teachers and staff can only impact students during the confines of the actual school day.

You may be wondering how to prioritize building parent capacity amid the sea of initiatives you have in front of you. In fact, if you are honest with yourself, perhaps building parent capacity is not even among your top priorities right now. If that is the case, I urge you to reframe how you look at the challenges your school faces through the lens of parent capacity. You will then begin to understand how your school/district functions as the center of the community. And the key that will change student outcomes is to seek out what community needs are not being met that either directly or indirectly affect a parent's ability to support their child, and to do so without judgment. You cannot serve needs you do not know. Once you know the needs, it will be easier to understand what resources to put in place, what to add to your strategic plan, and how to empower and connect parents while uplifting and serving them with dignity.

During my first principal position in the 1990s in St. Louis, I learned first-hand the power and importance of prioritizing parent capacity. I also learned the value of serving without judgment. At the time, I really had no idea of the underlying community needs we should address in order to successfully support student achievement, but after what happened on March 6, 2001, I realized our school could never be successful if I stayed ignorant to those needs any longer. Please note, this story contains some graphic content.

LIVED AND LEARNED

Serve Without Judgment

▶ In the spring of 2001, I was the principal at Clark School, a historic, poorly maintained, inner-city school that had cycled through several principals in the past three years. Clark was located on Union Blvd., which was essentially the dividing line, separating neighborhoods of extreme poverty on the north side and extreme wealth on the south side. On March 6, 2001, I started my day like any other, greeting my two parent liaisons, Joann and Debra, as I entered the school. Shortly after arriving on campus, I received a call from a police officer asking a question that no school leader wants to hear: "Did all of your students show up today?" My heart sank and my stomach lurched, because I knew what the officer meant by that question. A tragedy involving a child had occurred, and the police were working to figure out who that child was. I sent Joann racing through the building to collect attendance, and within minutes, just as Mr. Ellery Clark's fourth-grade class was about to leave for a field trip to the St. Louis Art Museum, I pulled him into my office. His student, Rodney McAllister, was absent. Within the hour, Rodney's mangled body was identified across the street in Ivory Perry Park by the homework in his pocket. Rodney's mother, a drug addict, never realizing he hadn't come home the night before, was awakened by the knock of police officers at her door coming to tell her about her son. We later learned that Rodney had been mauled to death by a pack of stray dogs. A person walking through the park that morning found Rodney's remains and had called the police. As I saw parents, I asked, "didn't you hear screaming?" And the answer was, "Yes, Dr. Anderson, we heard screaming all night. Something was suffering out there."

(Continued)

(Continued)

I was horrified and leaped to judgment, thinking how different the outcome of this situation may have been if people would have simply checked out their windows to see what was occurring. Reporters captured this response from parents in the stories that followed, as they recounted what was described as screams for help and cries that went unanswered all night. They reported on apathy, in which neighbors excused themselves from helping a child in need in literally their backyard (Simon, 2001).

Like many, I, too, jumped to judgment as they incarcerated his mother for neglect, and I asked neighboring parents why they didn't seek help. They quickly put me in my place and taught me a lesson that changed how I serve others. Their response gave me a sense of urgency to build the capacity of parents who live in and protect the neighborhoods and children in our community. "How dare you judge us, Doc? When we call the police, *if* they come, it will not be immediate." Some parents had actually called animal control in the days and weeks before to report the stray dogs throughout the neighborhood, but nothing had been done about it. They went on to say, "When we hear gunshots nightly, we lock our doors and hide under the bed hoping we are not next. And when we hear screams, we shut the blinds and close our eyes to what we do not want to be a witness to." They described the destructive principle of self-preservation held by communities who live in fear. The mantra "each to his own" is the backbone of self-preservation. Everyone suffers in the end.

Self-preservation is instinctual and built into the DNA of all living beings, particularly in people living in at-risk communities. However, as teachers and school and district leaders tasked with creating successful schools where students can thrive, we have to think beyond self-preservation and make decisions for the greater good of the community and the families we serve. Joseph Hill writes, "The principles of responsibility and security are important where leadership is concerned, as well, but as responsible citizens, defending and serving **for others** is the acceptable key to healthy forms of preservation" (Hill, 2015). Therefore, in order to preserve ourselves, we must realize that we are connected to one another, and we can only do well when others around us thrive and do well. As we mourned the loss of Rodney McAllister, it was clear to me that the only way to change these outcomes was to build parent capacity by thinking beyond the walls of our school—sharing messages of collective success, community preservation over self-preservation, and empowerment.

Our lived experience shapes us, and as we learn, we grow. The parents at Clark School described a community that I did not live in, resulting in a different perspective that I needed to more fully understand in order to help my school and my students be successful. As I reflected on the situation, I realized that they were right—how dare I judge or question? In the neighborhood I live in, police come when they are called and neighbors watch out for each other. As a result of Rodney's death, I realized two things: 1) I could not serve needs I did not know. Thus, my sneaker philosophy—walking the neighborhoods and meeting parents out at places within the community—was born; and 2) Parents have to see themselves as connected to the schools, and schools have to see themselves as the center of the community. No school improvement initiative will be sustainable unless capacity building is rooted in those two foundational pieces. Everyone benefits when we embrace the idea that parents are educators too. They are copartners in extending safety, compassion, and education in the neighborhood when the school day ends.

> ## My Sneaker Philosophy
>
> My sneaker philosophy is to come dressed for the work at hand, ready to meet people where they are. That means I wear sneakers every day as a feet-to-the-ground action plan in motion. I wear sneakers; I can't do the work I need to do in heels! To me, it's vital to be in classrooms and in the community every day in order to be most effective. Even though I serve as a superintendent, my role is to teach and learn in support of adults and students. Sometimes that's helping them see a path they didn't know they needed to be on or know that the path even existed for them.

BRINGING SCHOOLS TO THE CENTER OF THE COMMUNITY

To build parent capacity, we must change how we think about schools. Instead of schools being one aspect of the community—of equal importance as the neighborhoods, the places to eat or buy food, the places to purchase goods and services—we must think of schools as the center of the community around which the rest of the community can thrive.

A growing body of research suggests that placing schools at the center of the community has both a positive effect on student achievement (e.g., work efforts, habits, and attitudes; improved test scores and grades; lower dropout rates; and higher graduation rates) as well as success of the community itself (Henderson & Mapp, 2016). "Through partnerships with various community organizations, the school becomes a resource for community members to address their educational, physical, social, and emotional needs" (Simington, 2015) as well as helps target out-of-school barriers that children face (The Policy Circle, 2023). After all, it is very difficult for students to focus on academics and perform well in the classroom if their lives outside the classroom are chaotic. This holistic approach to the learning environment remodels the school into a multidimensional space to improve overall student well-being and builds the capacity of the families who support our students outside of school hours.

I like to think of the approach much like a relay race. When families drop off their children at school, they are passing the baton to the educators, saying, "Here you go! Please give my child the tools they need for success both inside the classroom and beyond." And at the end of the day when the children leave, we are passing the baton back to the families, saying, "Here you go! Let's keep this momentum moving forward." The greater the capacity parents have to perpetuate that momentum at home and in a community that is responsive to their needs, the greater our capacity is as educators to move the academic needle forward.

As we consider the implications of building parent capacity and shifting our mindset to understand schools as the center of the community, take some time to consider how this approach is different from the traditional model of school. Figure 1.1 provides some examples of the traditional approach versus the community-based approach.

FIGURE 1.1 Characteristics of a Traditional Approach vs. a Community-Based Approach

TRADITIONAL APPROACH	COMMUNITY-BASED APPROACH
• Activity based, determined by school	• Relationship based, based on mutual need
• Parents as individuals	• Parents as members of the community/collective
• Parents adapt to school rules and norms	• School holds necessary rules and norms but incorporates and reflects meaningful cultural and community values
• Parents follow school agenda and events	• Parents as leaders and collaborators in setting agendas and events
• Workshops provide information	• Workshops and training provide capacity building and personal growth
• Top-down, school to parent communication	• Meaningful conversation and two-way communication

SOURCE: Adapted from Warren et al. (2009).

Schools are more than institutions that produce graduates. Unlike transactional systems in business and in some factories, schools have interrelated parts that must work in concert with one another to serve the whole child. Schools are central to the transformational experiences within a community. Dr. Martin Luther King Jr. often quoted John Donne's famous words, "No man is an island, Entire of itself. Every man is a piece of the continent, a part of the main . . . The bell tolls for thee" (Donne, 1624). Communities and schools consist of collective voices that have the power to change generations, and their impact is in part dependent on their capacity to actively listen as involved parents, and become allies, advocates, and leaders moving with urgency in transforming schools and communities that will create a future filled with hope and prosperity.

In the months after Rodney's tragic death, parents from Clark School (later renamed Clark Accelerated Academy) and I advocated for stray dog legislation in St. Louis and it was passed. The legislation was signed at our school. It's an example of parent capacity being built through the call to act as a result of tragedy. People were empowered to do more to protect their community. Our school invested in ways we could do that together. This marked our collective shift to a more community-focused and relationship-based approach in St. Louis County.

That year, I started receiving anonymous Save the Children scarves and have since continued buying scarves. I wear them daily to work as a reminder of Rodney and of my commitment to build the capacity of parents and the community. Ultimately, lives depend on it. When Rodney's mother was released from prison, the community saw the need to expand services for addicts. We met with her, showed her Rodney's classroom, and loved on her as a grieving mother. We even created a memorial that has our fingerprints within it and planted a tree in remembrance. Now, more than twenty years later, Mr. Clark, Rodney's fourth-grade teacher, and I still meet and clean Ivory Perry Park every March. I still write letters lamenting how the city neglects the park (Anderson, 2016). The tree now has large branches that extend over the memorial—reminding us that we are an extension of one another. When we grow together as one parent and school community, we thrive together in support of the entire community.

LIVED AND LEARNED

It's Okay to Take a Moment

▶ Being an educator is challenging and often stressful, especially in situations involving tragedy and hardship. As superintendent, I often find myself in conversation with other educators about those challenges, and it's important to be honest and open when those feelings become overwhelming and you need to take a moment to reflect and catch your breath. We all need a moment from time to time. I certainly had those moments surrounding the tragedy of Rodney McAllister's death, and there have been many more since. But a moment needs to last a moment because too many other people are counting on you to make sure that their moments are filled with hope. So if you or others around you need to have a moment of sadness, of grief, of anger, or of frustration, it's important to have a system of self-care to ensure that those times in which you are emotionally drained remain only a moment. You must be able to recharge and be available to positively impact all the other moments around you.

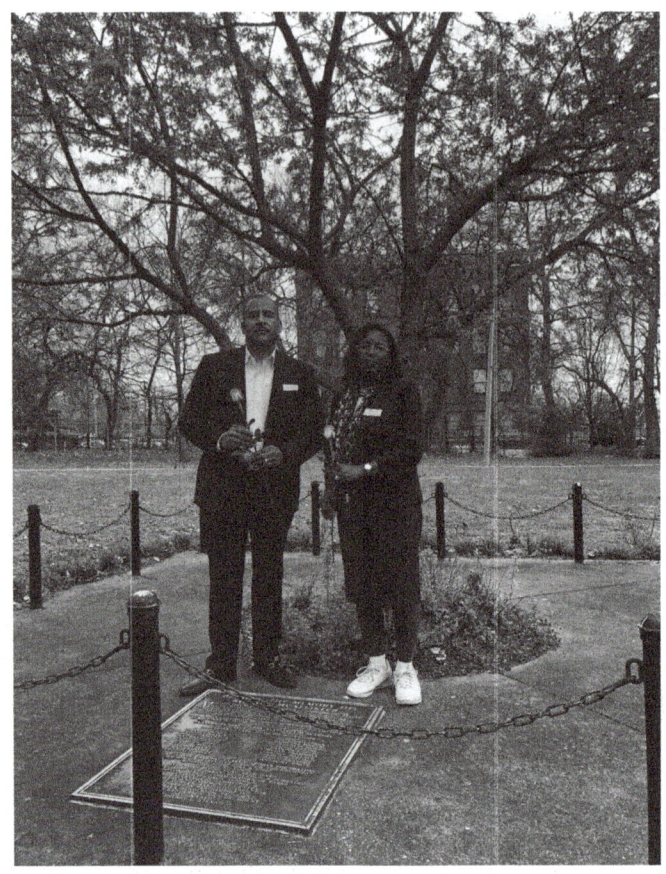

▶ Rodney's fourth-grade teacher, Mr. Clark, and Dr. Anderson at Rodney's memorial in 2015.

BUILDING PARENT CAPACITY IN ACTION

Dr. Aarion L. Gray is the Topeka Public Schools general director for instructional services and was principal at Randolph Elementary. Every day he welcomes students, parents, and staff as they enter school, and works to use every interaction as a teachable moment to empower others to change mindsets where needed. As an example, one year the school faced the challenge of parents dropping off their children unattended on campus well before the start of the school day. Dr. Gray, the school staff, and a group of parents quickly began a discussion about how to build parent capacity around this challenge. Every issue facing a student that a parent contributes to should be solved in partnership with parents when possible. While he was glad to see students coming to school, the dangers of leaving students outside before school began were clear to educators but not to the parents who were leaving their children. Dr. Gray's approach was not to criticize or scold families; rather, he planned to build their understanding. Some thought parents may lose their temper or use colorful language and asked whether he needed school resource officer staff to join him. Dr. Gray declined and instead chose to use patience, grace, and a smile to begin the conversation. He wanted to make families feel safe to share and listen, and the presence of a school resource officer might cause parents to be defensive or feel mistrusted.

The day he began his education campaign, Dr. Gray stood outside in the parking lot at sunrise, meeting parents who were dropping their children off before school was open. He took time to greet each individual, shake their hand, and share with them how glad he was they were present. With sincere support and compassion, he then spoke about his concerns for the safety of students left unattended.

I stopped at the school that morning to see how parents were receiving his approach and witnessed a mindset shift for each parent as he devoted time to listen, to learn, and to brainstorm ways to address the early morning childcare issues some faced, causing them to deliver their children hours before school began. Every parent loves their child, and Dr. Gray saw this as an opportunity to teach families about ways to help him better serve. He modeled for staff what capacity building looks like.

BUILDING PARENT CAPACITY REFLECTION

Think back to what you read throughout this chapter. Use these reflection questions to consider your own school or district and the role you play in building parent capacity.

1. How do you see yourself (What role do you play in the school where you serve)?

2. How do teachers see themselves and how do they view the school?

3. How do parents see themselves and how do they view the school?

Take some time to reflect on your learning and plan for action in your next steps.

WHAT?

Summarize your learning and key takeaways from this chapter.

SO WHAT?

Record ideas about how your key takeaways apply to you, your school, and/or your district.

NOW WHAT?

Based on your key takeaways, plan your next steps for moving forward in this area.

CHAPTER 2

Building Relationships With Parents

"The question is not what you look at—but how you look and whether you see."

—Thoreau (1851)

On the surface the idea of parental involvement and parental engagement may seem very similar. After all, a variety of research studies show that increasing both parental involvement in school and parental engagement with school can produce positive student academic achievement and motivation and even have a positive impact on students' social and emotional skills (e.g., Epstein, 2001; Henderson & Mapp, 2002; Stanford, 2023).

But if we look a bit more closely, we will see that parental involvement is transactional whereas parental engagement has the power to be transformational. A transactional relationship involves telling and possibly some teaching. Whereas a transformational relationship focuses on involving parents, and when teaching happens it happens through involvement. Think back to Figure 1.1. The traditional approach puts schools in control of the power. Schools set the tone, choose the activities, and distribute important information, and then tell parents how they can volunteer and when they are supposed to show up on campus. Communication is typically one-way and can often take a disciplinary focus. This is parent involvement—how parents can contribute, volunteer, or donate money to what the school says is needed most. Although we certainly want many families to attend events or celebrations on campus, just because a lot of people show up doesn't necessarily mean that families are engaged with the school.

The community-based approach focuses more on relationship building and sharing power to build collective efficacy and affirm different cultural norms and practices. Thus, parent engagement becomes about listening, two-way communication, collective decision-making and problem solving, and building parent capacity as leaders and organizers within the school, their families, and the greater community. The emphasis of parent and family engagement over parent involvement is now also part of federal legislation. The Every Student Succeeds Act (ESSA) calls for the sharing of power between families and those who educate their children with the term *engagement* preferred over parent *involvement* (Every Student Succeeds Act of 2015 [ESSA], 2015).

Author and educator Larry Ferlazzo paints a clear picture of the distinction between involvement and engagement. He says, "A school striving for family involvement often leads with its mouth—identifying projects, needs, and goals and then telling parents how they can contribute. A school striving for parent engagement, on the other hand, tends to lead with its ears—listening to what parents think, dream, and worry about. The goal of family engagement is not to serve clients but to gain partners" (Ferlazzo, 2011).

Heather Weiss (Walsh, 2015), director of the Harvard Family Research Project, furthers this idea. She explains that family engagement "is not a single event." Rather, "It is a shared responsibility in which regular two-way communication insures that the student is on track to meet grade-level requirements. It is founded on trust and mutual respect and acknowledges that all families have the goals, values, and skills to help their children succeed from preschool through high school, and beyond."

Thus, in order to create meaningful partnerships with parents, we must strive for engagement rather than involvement. To do that, we must more fully understand who the families are that we serve in our schools so that we can meet them where they are and walk alongside them.

UNDERSTANDING TODAY'S PARENTS

The diversity of students in today's classrooms reflects today's parents who are a heterogeneous mix of backgrounds, cultures, ages, and perspectives. In addition to the traditional image of a parent that may represent the majority of parents served in many schools, parents today also include the extended families who have stepped in to care for a child in need, teenagers who have children while in school as children themselves, foster parents, parents who are recent immigrants, and many more. But no matter the demographic at your schools, one thing that all of today's parents face is a world of unparalleled change.

In the wake of the COVID-19 pandemic and with prevalence of social media and other technologies, parenting today is very different than it was even twenty years ago. According to a Pew Research Center study (Minkin & Horowitz, 2023), 40 percent of parents with children under the age of eighteen are extremely or very worried that their children will struggle with anxiety or depression, followed by 35 percent who are similarly concerned about their children being bullied. Parental worries also vary by race and ethnicity. For example, Black and Hispanic parents tend to worry most about their children getting in trouble with police; getting shot or attacked; being bullied; having problems with drugs or alcohol; or teen pregnancy. These concerns also overlap with parent's income levels, with lower-income parents sharing higher concern for their children in those areas than middle- or high-level income parents.

While parents of different income and racial groups may have different perspectives based on their cultural and socioeconomic experiences according to the Pew study, they largely share similar goals and aspirations for their children, with large majorities saying, "it's extremely or very important to them that their children be honest, ethical and hardworking as adults and that they be financially independent and have jobs or careers they enjoy" (Minkin & Horowitz, 2023). Further, 87 percent of parents say it's one of the most, if not the most important aspect of their lives.

Thus, as we consider how to best partner with parents and increase their collective capacity, we must examine how to lessen or alleviate the barriers that prevent parents from being engaged in their children's lives and schooling and walk alongside our parents to listen to them, build their capacity, and help them see their voice matters.

BUILDING PARENT CAPACITY THROUGH AN ASSET-BASED APPROACH

Given the research that indicates an overwhelming majority of adults say that being a parent is the most important aspect of their lives, we must focus on building parents up using their strengths and focusing on their intrinsic desires to see their children succeed and refrain from labeling or categorizing parents based on their deficits.

In order to build parent capacity, educators must embrace an asset-based mindset where we seek first to understand, focus on the strengths that parents and the community possess, and look at the challenges as opportunities for growth and change. Simply put, asset-based thinking unlocks potential while deficit mindset highlights inadequacies. And in the context of family engagement, this means understanding and truly believing that "all caregivers are capable of supporting student learning and development and engaging as equal partners in the education of their children and the improvement of schools" (Mapp & Bergman, 2021). Consider these alternative perspectives to some common deficit thinking:

Deficit mindset: Parents are combative.

Alternative perspective: Parents aren't naturally combative. Perhaps they had negative experiences with teachers or with the school system and don't yet trust that educators have the best interest of their child at heart. And even more challenging, what if the school where they had these negative experiences is the same school their child is now attending? Or perhaps they are currently going through life experiences that are causing significant stress, which results in an aggressive attitude. Their frustration may be misplaced, but that doesn't mean they are always combative.

Deficit mindset: Parents don't want to help their children with their homework.

Alternative perspective: Parents may want to help their children with homework. But perhaps they aren't home in the afternoons and evenings because they are working or they have limited literacy or English skills, which prevents them from being involved or gaining assistance to avoid embarrassment.

Deficit mindset: Parents don't want to show up on campus.

Alternative perspective: Parents may want to be present at school, however the barriers of inflexible work hours or reliable transportation may impact their ability to support their child by being present. Even with offering what we may view as a resource to remove barriers, such as a free bus pass from the school, if the distance between walking to the bus and traveling to school and back requires more time than the event or school meeting, what educators intended to be a resource may not actually remove the barrier impacting parent engagement.

> *Our parents and students do not need saviors; they do not need heroes. They are the heroes in their own story.*

When we seek to understand, we improve how we serve. We simply cannot serve needs we do not know and there's often more to the story than we originally may have thought. Our parents and students do not need saviors; they do not need heroes. They are the heroes in their own story. What parents do need, however, are partners who see the many gifts they bring as assets that strengthen and uplift the organization with an added diverse perspective. In the words of Thurgood Marshall, "None of us got where we are solely by pulling ourselves up by our bootstraps. We got here because somebody—a parent, a teacher, an Ivy League crony, or a few nuns—bent down and helped us pick up our boots." Our communities and our families are the biggest asset we have, but we need to know who they are and understand their cultures and backgrounds in order to be successful. We can't build parent capacity if we believe fundamental untruths about who our parents are, what they represent, or what is important to them. This is especially important for educators who serve families of different backgrounds or cultures than themselves. According to enrollment statistics from the 2020–2021 school year (National Center for Education Statistics [NCES], 2022), more than 80 percent of public school educators are white, yet they serve an increasingly diverse student population. Nationwide, public schools serve nearly 50 million students, which include:

- 22.4 million white students;
- 14.1 million Hispanic students;
- 7.4 million Black students;
- 2.7 million Asian students;
- 2.3 million students of two or more races;
- 0.5 million American Indian and Alaska Native students; and
- 0.2 million Pacific Islander students.

In addition to using an asset-based approach with the thoughts and judgments we make about people and situations, an asset-based approach can positively affect the language we use. Imagine being a student who is only viewed through their deficits: as a student who is disruptive and noisy and can't sit still. Now consider how it would feel to be the same student but viewed through an asset-based lens instead: as a student who is full of energy and creativity and sees things differently than others. These questions, compiled by Mapp and Bergman (2021), provide a good lens through which to evaluate the language we use with and about our students and parents.

Does my language . . .

- Correct assumptions others may have about the person or group of people I am referring to?
- Avoid stereotypes about the people, places, and communities I am referencing?
- Assign responsibility for inequities to the system(s) that create and perpetuate those inequities, rather than assigning blame to individuals?
- Humanize the person or group of people, rather than defining them by one or several characteristics?
- Use descriptors of people or communities that are relevant and necessary for understanding what I am trying to convey?
- Contribute to a better or more holistic understanding of the people or communities I am discussing?

When we become intentional about our language and our mindset, asset-based thinking can transform how we teach and how we serve the families in our communities. But if we view capacity building as "someone else's problem" rather than through an asset-based lens of partnerships, we automatically create silos between those whom we have the privilege of serving and ourselves.

A PYRAMID OF PARENT ENGAGEMENT

From my experience, as we continue to employ an asset-based lens, there are a variety of ways in which parents typically demonstrate their engagement in schools. Some parents are leaders, while others act as allies or as advocates. Still others present themselves more as listeners and participators. All groups of parents are needed to encourage, support, and educate others to look from new perspectives. All parents can challenge us to develop new approaches and are needed to help us transform schools and communities. Some parents can hold multiple roles, but that isn't necessary for school or district success. In fact, I like to think of these roles as a pyramid, with fewer and fewer parents holding those roles the closer to the top of the pyramid we get.

FIGURE 2.1 The Pyramid of Parental Engagement

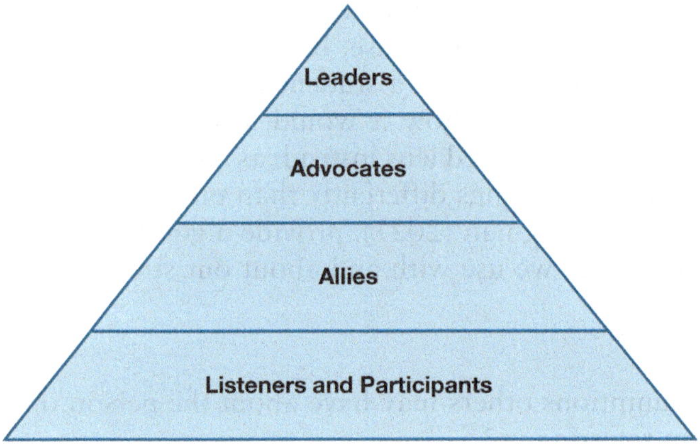

If we think back to Linda Brown and the parents who were involved in *Brown v. Board of Education*, those parents were courageous advocates for their children and communities, and the actions they took to lead the way in desegregating schools were a critical part of the Civil Rights Movement. They functioned as allies for each other as parents and listened to the needs of others as they brought forth examples of unfair education practices in their communities.

Parents as Listeners and Participants

Not all parents have the physical time or home stability to be able to be on campus or participate in school-day activities. However, that doesn't mean that they can't be engaged in the school and the school lives of their children. Research shows the primary motivation for parents to become involved is the belief that their actions will improve their children's learning and well-being

(Centers for Disease Control and Prevention, 2019). Research further shows that students who have parents who are engaged in their education and school lives are more likely to have higher grades and test scores, better behavior, and enhanced social skills. Students are also less likely to smoke cigarettes, drink alcohol, become pregnant, be physically inactive, or be emotionally distressed (Centers for Disease Control and Prevention, 2019).

Two of the most important ways to engage parents is through consistent communication and listening. Parents will become engaged and stay engaged when they know they are informed about the happenings and the resources available at the school and that their voice is important—should they choose to use it. To learn about strategies for effective listening and communication, see Chapter 3.

You can recognize parent listeners and participants because they . . .

- Stay informed of things going on but may not take full advantage of available resources
- Limit participation to parent conferences, donating classroom items (snacks or school supplies), and giving to fundraising efforts
- Typically attend large events and activities for the social aspects

Parents as Allies

The word *ally* comes from the word *alliance*, meaning a bond or connection between people or groups. Parents who are allies are those prepared to walk alongside a mission and a vision they believe in and take action for that mission and vision when necessary. Parents who are allies also function as a support system for one another. Imagine if there were no alliance built between the parents who became the plaintiffs in the case for Linda Brown. Transforming the hearts and minds of a nation focused on school desegregation required those parents to work together and move forward with a common goal and purpose. It is important to note that parent allies may take different forms. Parent allies focused exclusively on academic outcomes outlined by the school would be engaged in a different way than parent allies who were focused on supporting the whole child, which may include mental health needs or social supports critical to school success.

You can recognize parent allies because they . . .

- Stand alongside the school staff and other parents
- Serve as critical friends available to assist with initiatives, projects, and activities in support of a larger vision
- Typically are highly involved in PTO/PTA meetings or other activities and frequently volunteer on campus

Parents as Advocates

Parent advocates are those who will support their child in gaining the services and supports needed to excel in school. Schools function best when families and educators are aligned and advocate together in the best interest of students. The issue at times can be determining what's best for the student at school, which can look very different from what's best for a child at home. If there are unmet student needs, we need parents to advocate by sharing those needs and helping schools identify the best ways to support those children. Parent advocates understand that the needs of their child are just as important as the needs of other children in the school and work toward the collective success and well-being.

There is a divide between parents with firsthand experience of US schools and the rest of the country that has gotten worse since the onset of the pandemic and rise in political polarization. Despite downward trends in academic performance, according to polling, 76 percent of parents believe their K–12 students are receiving a quality education. However, just 36 percent of adults overall say they are satisfied with K–12 education (Rubin, 2023). Advocacy is needed to change this perception gap. To begin this journey, schools need to provide messaging to families as well as across the community. The messaging should define advocacy and explain the many ways that schools are educational advocates for children and families, including sharing resources and providing needed services.

Building trust and respect between parents and educators is the foundation from which to grow a strong parent and school advocacy relationship. When parents see educators as their child's advocate, their willingness to share information with the school (be it positive or critical), to accept needed services, and to further participate in the educational process occurs at much higher levels. When parents feel they have to advocate for their children in protection from the school, everything the school does may be viewed as suspicious and the school is not viewed as a partner. To avoid this, schools can provide advocacy workshops, family handbooks, and information to families as partners with the joint goal of supporting all children. The ultimate goal is for parents to not only advocate *with* the school on behalf of children and families but *independent* of the school on behalf of children and families to bring others alongside the work of collective success. As we give more parents a voice, the more they spread the word among other parents and community organizations that the school is a trusted partner and a resource for the community.

You can recognize parent advocates because they . . .

- Are prepared to take a position on an issue or topic and will share their reasons for their stance

- Engage in broader issues that affect the school/students and that they care about (e.g., special education resources, gun legislation, equitable teaching practices)

- Willingly attend meetings, gather information as a contributor, or advocate for a cause or issue but won't take the lead role in organization or speaking out publicly

Parents as Leaders

In order for true school transformation to exist, parent voices must be given power and be present in decision-making. For example, rather than being passive participants at parent workshops, parent leaders should be able to influence the types of topics that are presented and other programming that exists for parents at the school. Parent leaders not only galvanize other parents but can also serve as relational bridges to help close the gap that may exist between teachers and the greater parent population. Parent leaders are likely to naturally show themselves on campus, because they tend to incorporate the qualities of parent allies and parent advocates, but with a seemingly innate ability to bring others along with them and to convince others to join as allies for initiatives, programs, or other school activities. However, it is also possible to train parents through specific programs or initiatives to build their capacity and leadership abilities.

You can recognize parent leaders because they . . .

- Willingly lead a group

- Share the collective voices as one united voice with themselves as the spokesperson

- Feel empowered to take action alongside others or independently if the situation or issue requires and make decisions

- Serve typically as PTO/PTA presidents, community organizers, or group leaders

- Are outspoken on issues of growth and change for the betterment of families, the community, and students

- Will be disruptors of progress should they not be given positive and productive ways to use their leadership skills for the betterment of others and the school

LIVED AND LEARNED

Let Parents Lead

▶ The idea of having a District Parent Advisory Committee is nothing new. These types of committees typically comprise of a group of involved parents who meet with superintendents and other district leaders to learn about what's going on in the district and then take that information back to disseminate at their own school. This is all well and good, but don't just limit your parent advisory group to acting as goodwill ambassadors. As invested parents, they can do so much more.

In the districts I have led, the Parent Advisory Committee functions in the traditional sense but also chooses an area of focus each year. In Topeka, at the beginning of the year, the group meets and selects a topic of interest for the committee. The topic is truly a reflection of something parents think is important for our schools to pay attention to. Recently the topic was restorative practices, but other topics through the years have been classroom technology, after-school enrichment, and mental health resources. Once the topic is selected, the group does extensive research to better understand it. They often look at different schools or districts to get examples of what others do, as well as conduct surveys and gather information in order to get ideas about what should be done in our district. At the end of the year, they present their findings and recommendations to the school board and then we act on those recommendations. Through this process, parents are given voice and choice, and are empowered to truly influence how our district approaches important topics in education. Parents also become more invested in their schools, as they see the results of their recommendations enacted. It's this type of work that transforms parents into leaders not only at their schools but also in their families and their communities, and as their capacity and self-efficacy grows through this work they have the confidence to take on new leadership roles in the community, as well. In fact, several of the parents who served on our Parent Advisory Council in Topeka have since gone on to sit on the school board and some have even served as school board president.

BUILDING PARENT CAPACITY THROUGH THE THREE Rs

Regardless of whether a parent acts as a leader, ally, advocate, or listener, developing rapport, relationship, and respect is necessary in order to impact and engage any parent in school. Dr. Hollie (2017) references these as the three Rs in his work related to culturally responsive teaching practices. And while his focus is on students, this approach is just as impactful and important when working with parents.

Rapport is the special connection between the teacher and the parent and student. When rapport is present, both parties can understand each other's feelings and effectively communicate with one another.

Relationship is all about trust. When a teacher has taken time to build a relationship with a parent and student, they will respond differently to the teacher. Parents and students respond differently to adults they know and trust. To help educators check their beliefs and assumptions about how they go about building trust with all families, Mapp and Bergman (2021) offer the questions below, rooted in the four key elements for relational trust— respect, integrity, competence, and personal regard.

- Am I seeking input from, and do I listen to and value, what all families have to say? (Respect)
- Am I demonstrating to all families that I am competent and that I see them as competent and valuable caretakers? (Competence)
- Do I keep my word with families? (Integrity)
- Do I show families that I value and care about them as people? (Personal Regard)

Respect must be in place. Parents and students need to see educators as capable of delivering knowledge to all students. Educators need to recognize that all parents and students are capable of high achievement.

"When schools build partnerships with families that respond to their concerns, honor their contributions, and share their power, they succeed in sustaining connections that are aimed at improving student achievement" (Family Strengthening Policy Center, 2004). Here are some organizations that can help schools develop the three Rs and build strong partnerships with parents.

Parents as Teachers (PAT): This is a national evidence-based program focused on empowering parents by partnering with them to "build strong communities, thriving families and children who are healthy, safe, and learning" so they are ready for school (Parents as Teachers, 2024). PAT provides free services to families with children prenatal through kindergarten, and PAT Educators support, teach, and connect with families to help them understand and build their role as a child's first educator. As these goals are realized and parent capacity increases, Topeka's National Blue Ribbon PAT Educators are often seen as allies and advocates among parents within the school.

National Alliance on Mental Illness (NAMI): NAMI is a national program focused on mental health. Most cities have a NAMI organization that can provide free resources and training. One way they do this is through their Parents & Teachers as Allies program, which is an in-service training focused on helping school professionals and families better understand mental illness early warning signs in children and adolescents (National Alliance on Mental Illness [NAMI], 2014). As parents become better informed of the early

Suicide is the third leading cause of death in teens. Recognizing this statistic, in Topeka, we use resources from organizations that offer free services to the community, such as the National Alliance on Mental Illness (NAMI Kansas). This national organization provides resources and services across the community for families and is an immediate network to other parents who may have similar needs.

warning signs of mental illness, they are better prepared to act as advocates for new or improved programs, resources, or services within their schools or districts. In Topeka, our district coordinator of social work collaborates with NAMI as a free resource to our families.

State and Locally Driven Programs: Some states have invested in their own parent engagement programs, such as Parents as Allies in Pennsylvania. In this program, twenty-two school districts partnered with HundrEd (an independent organization that seeks to identify impactful and scalable education innovations and help education providers to implement them worldwide) and used Parents as Allies, a family engagement program focused on developing parents who are trusted partners. They share, "Based on the Brookings Institution research, schools that have strong relational trust are ten times more likely to have really good educational outcomes" (HundrEd, 2023). They teach the school how to build trust with parents and share various strategies that can be used. These types of programs can be highly effective when used within a system that will remain long term.

LIVED AND LEARNED

When Families Can't, We MUST

▶ No matter the income or social status, not every child has an adult at home who wants to be or has the capacity to be fully engaged in schools. And with the growing number of homeless families, extended family members serving as guardians, and foster parents, schools have to be ready to meet any parent (or adult functioning as a parent) where they are and serve the family to the best of their ability. It is also important to make sure that staff are trained to know the signs of children whose parents may suffer from addiction or struggle with mental health. In those instances, we have the opportunity—and I would argue the obligation—to step in and be the parent in lieu of the parent and to provide when parents can't or don't or won't.

On any given day, that means that if a child comes to school with poor hygiene or in need of clothing, we provide that resource as a safe haven for them. It they're hungry, we provide nourishment and extra resources for home. Educators and schools must step in daily to serve those social service needs that must be addressed in order for learning to occur. And in extreme cases where tragic events impact a child or their family—like in the case of Rodney McAllister—we may even need to attend memorial services or create opportunities for remembrance to enable the community to grieve and begin the healing process together, because our schools are at the center of the communities in which we serve and are impacted by everything that surrounds them.

BUILDING PARENT CAPACITY THROUGH EFFECTIVE FEEDBACK

Researcher Hattie (2008) describes visible learning as the process of becoming an evaluator of your own practice to enhance what you do. As we build rapport, relationship, and respect with parents, growing their capacity also requires educators to help parents think critically and assess their own parenting practices. In a 2012 edition of *Educational Leadership*, Hattie and other leading educators described proven ways to provide feedback to students. If we replace students with parents in those key takeaways, we can see simple ways to help parents become visible learners in their own parenting practices.

1. **Feedback is not advice, praise, or evaluation. Feedback is about how we are doing.**

   Parents do not necessarily have a measure of effective parenting, and it's important to remember that they generally compare themselves to what they have seen or what they experienced in their own childhoods. Therefore, in order to build parent capacity, we must focus on giving parents feedback and provide opportunities for them to build their capacity as parents and as members of their school and community. One way to do this is to provide parents with an opportunity for reflection after attending parent workshops. As an "exit ticket," consider having parents write a brief personal reflection comparing their practices to what they viewed and learned about, and then set a personal goal relating to a practice they want to stop doing or start doing as a result. This type of self-assessment often brings about a greater sense of self-awareness and opens the door to seek assistance or support, if needed.

2. **When parents know the school and classroom is a safe space to make mistakes, they are more likely to use the feedback for learning.**

   In order for families to share, ask questions, and feel free from judgment, the school and the classroom must be seen as a safe space. This allows for families to become vulnerable with the school and grow as parents. When fear is removed, true freedom to learn and grow fills the space. To assess whether a safe environment exists at your school, it is a good idea to administer a school climate survey. This can be done every year or every other year depending on student turnover rates at your school. Figure 2.2 shows an example of a school climate survey— you can also find a full-size version in Appendix A.

FIGURE 2.2   Sample School Climate Survey

SCHOOL CLIMATE SURVEY

Dear Families,

We want our school to be the best it can be. Please complete this survey and tell us what you think are the school's strong points and where we can improve. Your honest comments and ideas are very welcome. If you would like to help tally and analyze the results, please let us know.

The Family and Community Involvement Action Team

No	SCHOOL ENVIRONMENT
1	**The people make me feel welcome when I walk into this school.** ◯ Always ◯ Almost Always ◯ Sometimes ◯ Rarely ◯ Never
2	**The school environment makes me feel welcome when I walk into this school.** ◯ Always ◯ Almost Always ◯ Sometimes ◯ Rarely ◯ Never
3	**I am treated with respect at the school.** ◯ Always ◯ Almost Always ◯ Sometimes ◯ Rarely ◯ Never
4	**I see my cultural heritage reflected in aspects of the building/campus itself.** ◯ Always ◯ Almost Always ◯ Sometimes ◯ Rarely ◯ Never
5	**Students at the school are treated fairly no matter what their race or cultural background.** ◯ Always ◯ Almost Always ◯ Sometimes ◯ Rarely ◯ Never
6	**I feel welcome at school-related activities or functions.** ◯ Always ◯ Almost Always ◯ Sometimes ◯ Rarely ◯ Never

No	PROBLEM SOLVING
7	**I have a good working relationship with my child/children's teacher(s).** ◯ Always ◯ Almost Always ◯ Sometimes ◯ Rarely ◯ Never
8	**I can talk to the school principal or other administrators when I need to.** ◯ Always ◯ Almost Always ◯ Sometimes ◯ Rarely ◯ Never
9	**I know who to go to when I have specific questions.** ◯ Always ◯ Almost Always ◯ Sometimes ◯ Rarely ◯ Never

No	PROBLEM SOLVING (CONT.)
10	The school has a clear process for addressing my concerns. ◯ Always ◯ Almost Always ◯ Sometimes ◯ Rarely ◯ Never
11	If the school can't help me, I know they will refer me to someone who can. ◯ Always ◯ Almost Always ◯ Sometimes ◯ Rarely ◯ Never
12	I feel welcomed and encouraged to make suggestions for improvement or share new ideas. ◯ Always ◯ Almost Always ◯ Sometimes ◯ Rarely ◯ Never

No	COMMUNICATION
13	I feel informed about available resources at school. ◯ Always ◯ Almost Always ◯ Sometimes ◯ Rarely ◯ Never
14	I feel informed about events and activities happening at school. ◯ Always ◯ Almost Always ◯ Sometimes ◯ Rarely ◯ Never
15	I feel informed about ways to get involved/volunteer at school. ◯ Always ◯ Almost Always ◯ Sometimes ◯ Rarely ◯ Never
16	A translator is available easily, if needed. ◯ Always ◯ Almost Always ◯ Sometimes ◯ Rarely ◯ Never
17	Communication is regular and timely. ◯ Always ◯ Almost Always ◯ Sometimes ◯ Rarely ◯ Never
18	Staff at the school consult me and other families before making important decisions. ◯ Always ◯ Almost Always ◯ Sometimes ◯ Rarely ◯ Never
19	I understand the school rules and expectations around student behavior, academics, and dress. ◯ Always ◯ Almost Always ◯ Sometimes ◯ Rarely ◯ Never

(Continued)

(Continued)

No	SATISFACTION				
20	**I am satisfied with the quality of the school.**				
	◯ Always	◯ Almost Always	◯ Sometimes	◯ Rarely	◯ Never
21	**I would recommend this school to other families and friends.**				
	◯ Always	◯ Almost Always	◯ Sometimes	◯ Rarely	◯ Never

No	OPEN RESPONSE
22	**What is the school doing that is most helpful to you as a parent?**
23	**What changes would you like to see at the school?**

Thank you for your participation!

Please return this survey to:

SOURCE: Adapted from School Climate Survey from Henderson et al. (2007).

Once school climate surveys are collected and responses are analyzed, it is important to consider changes that respond to the feedback. Changes I have seen as a result of climate surveys include providing additional parent workshops on requested topics (money management, early literacy, etc.) and adding family centers around campus. "Special places in schools where family members can meet, plan, and implement programs, family centers are also places where school staff and community volunteers are invited to collaborate in support of children's academic and social development. Particularly important to participants in the family center was the *designation* of a special place in schools for families. . . . 'A place of their own' for parents in schools . . . which represents a significant symbolic and structural change in a school's relationship with families" (Henderson et al., 2007).

3. **The feedback parents give teachers can be more valuable than what teachers give parents.**

   Listening to learn and adjusting based on feedback is important. Schools often collect parent feedback through school climate surveys or welcome surveys, but this is typically only once or twice a year. In order for parents to share feedback throughout the year, provide additional, ongoing collection methods so the school can address challenges or concerns that arise. Possible solutions include a physical suggestion box in a central location, an online feedback portal, or a feedback form on the district or school web page.

   It is also important to be open and welcoming for parent feedback to come to the school and teachers through nontraditional routes, such as through leaders at local community-based organizations (church leaders, after-school program coordinators, neighborhood association leaders, etc.). If a school has not yet gained full trust or buy-in with parents or doesn't have an established method to gather feedback and ideas from parents, utilizing those community leaders who parents *do* communicate with regularly can go a long way in establishing deeper rapport and relationship in the community so that gradually parents see the school as a trusted partner where their voice and opinions matter and will be acted on in a positive way.

4. **When we immediately share grades as part of our feedback, parents read as far as the grade.**

   During conversations or conferences with parents, it is important for educators to focus on student growth and share evidence of learning and progress through work samples, observational checklists, or anecdotal notes. Labels matter, and once a parent feels their child is labeled as struggling or failing, defenses come up and discussion often minimizes. Depending on parents' experiences with school, they could even shut down completely assuming that there isn't a road toward success or that the teacher isn't really interested in helping their child. Ultimately, parents want their child to succeed, and before sharing a grade, growth information and artifacts of learning should be the starting point for the conversation. A conference checklist can be used to encourage teachers to adequately prepare and reflect on parent conferences. See a sample in Figure 2.3 as well as a larger checklist in Appendix B.

FIGURE 2.3   Sample Conference Checklist

Conference Checklist

Before the Conference

1. **Notify parents about the following:**

   - Purpose

   - Time and location options

   - Length of time

   - Childcare or transportation options

2. **Prepare:**

   - Gather official necessary documents (report card, progress report, etc.)

   - Gather student work samples

   - Gather other materials (observational checklists/rubrics, anecdotal notes, etc.)

   - Gather input from student (if appropriate)

   - Schedule additional conference participants, if appropriate (translator, administrator, etc.)

   - Plan what to say and questions to ask (avoid specialized educational terms)

3. **Plan agenda:**

   - Create plan for the flow of the conference

   - Emphasize cooperation (what can we do together?)

4. **Arrange environment:**

   - Place seating away from desk

   - Make sure seating space is clear from clutter or other school materials

   - Make sure all materials are easily accessible and easily seen/discussed together

   - Make sure there is privacy

   - Make sure room feels welcoming and inviting

During the Conference

1. **Welcome.** Establish rapport and open opportunity to share.

2. **Set terms.** State the purpose of the conference, remind of time limits, encourage note taking and questions, and mention options for follow-up after the conference.

3. **Lead with the positive.** Share the child's major strengths, both academic and social. Share what you enjoy most and what makes child unique.

4. **Open the floor.** Ask parents to share any comments, information, or observations they see or ask any initial questions.

5. **Show.** Share evidence of child's academic and/or social growth.

6. **Listen.** Ask for feedback from parents. Look for verbal and nonverbal clues about how things are going and invite additional questions.

7. **Share opportunities for growth and develop action plan.** Share areas for academic or social growth. Be specific. Develop an action plan focusing on one or two areas with action items for both parents and teacher(s).

8. **Summarize.** Summarize the conversation and plan next meeting time to check in on action plan.

9. **End with the positive.** Express confidence in the child's ability to meet goals and continue growth. Share excitement and appreciation for parent-teacher partnership to support child's growth.

After the Conference

1. **Review** the action plan and make sure you strategically integrate agreed-on steps into instruction.

2. **Share** action plan information with other school staff, resource teachers, etc., if needed, especially if other teachers support the child outside your classroom.

3. **Send** a follow-up thank you note or email to the parents.

4. **Mark calendar** with the planned follow-up date/timeline.

SOURCE: Adapted from Henderson et al. (2007).

5. **Effective feedback on learning comes while the learning is still occurring.**

To give a simple view of what learning by doing looks like, think about things you have learned, such as riding a bike or cooking. I can recall learning the most about cooking when my mother could guide me while making the dish itself. Parents and students are the same way (Ruelle, 2019). There's a quote by Aristotle that says, "For the things we have to learn before we can do them, we learn by doing them" (Aristotle, 350 BCE). Connections in the brain grow and multiply as it experiences learning, and the more experiences parents can get with activities that result in them practicing what's being learned the more their capacity to apply those skills or engage in those activities outside of the school setting becomes. Learning is strengthened even further when parents set measurable goals for themselves that can be obtained throughout the course of the school year. Ways to involve families in learning while doing include but are not limited to:

- Involving parents as volunteers who engage in the true classroom learning process. This gives parents new techniques or strategies they can use at home.

- Providing classes or workshops based on parents' suggestions taught in a hands-on learning approach, such as creating meals on a budget or activities to support early language development. These classes or workshops can be taught by other parents or local experts on the workshop topic (e.g., a high school cooking teacher or a local restaurant partner).

- Creating parent and child stations in classrooms and throughout the school, which allows parents to read to children, engage in math and literacy stations, and other learning experiences.

POWERFUL PARENTS IN ACTION

The experiences and resilience of parents is an asset that can provide a new perspective to educators and can increase the committment of the parent to advocate in various ways.

One inspirational parent whose resilience and strenth empowered and fueled her committment to the school and community is Former Mayor Michelle De La Isla. She served as an ally, advocate, and leader partnering with schools and community-focused organizations as a single mother who became Topeka's first Afro-Latina mayor, opening the door for the second Latino mayor elected after her.

Her story of resilience leaving her home in Puerto Rico at age seventeen and becoming a new mother at twenty is a story that many young mothers and limited English proficient parents could relate to. The future Mayor De La Isla began attending college at Wichita State because the school offered financial assistance and vocational training, both of which Michelle knew she would need in order to succeed. After graduation, she began working with Upward Bound, which "provides limited-income and potential first-generation college students with the opportunity to improve their academic, social and personal skills while preparing for a post-secondary education" (Upward Bound Wichita Prep, 2024). The program specifically partnered with high school students attending Wichita Prep, and Michelle's story allowed for others in her similar situation to see hope. Soon after, she moved to Topeka and through a human reources job, she gave other first-generation college graduates a chance. As a parent, Mayor De La Isla told her story of resilience and opportunity, making her an ally, a true friend to many parents who could relate to her story. She used every opportunity to build her own capacity or have it built by others so the opportunities could serve as a stairway to a brighter future. Mayor De La Isla was a leader who helped organize parents and showed through her own story and her visibility in schools what an ally, advocate, and leader looked like. As a result, she inspired trust and was elected as the first Latina to serve as mayor, which forever changed the history of Topeka.

POWERFUL PARENTS REFLECTION

Think back to what you read throughout this chapter. Use these reflection questions to consider your own school or district and the role you play in building parent capacity.

1. Does your school or district place a priority on parents as partners? Why or why not?

2. What do you want everyone to be able to say about the relationships between your school/district and your parents?

3. Do parents see themselves as partners in education to meet the needs of the students who you serve? If yes, what are you doing well that enables parents to see themselves this way. If not, why do you think that is and what could be done differently?

4. Does the school create a positive climate for parents? If not, why do you think that is and what could be done differently?

5. Are there partnerships with parents that are not occurring that could be? If yes, what are they and how could those move forward?

Take some time to reflect on your learning and plan for action in your next steps.

WHAT?

Summarize your learning and key takeaways from this chapter.

SO WHAT?

Record ideas about how your key takeaways apply to you, your school, and/or your district.

NOW WHAT?

Based on your key takeaways, plan your next steps for moving forward in this area.

CHAPTER 3

Walking the Talk

"A leader is one who knows the way, goes the way, and shows the way."

—Maxwell (2014)

Walk the talk is about putting your words into action and showing that you mean what you say, and as a school or district leader this type of authenticity is pivotal to building parent capacity and creating opportunities for school to function as the center of the community.

Educational leaders are vital to the overall philosophy and integrity of school and district culture. "With impactful educational leadership, schools develop into student-driven incubators of learning and education zones for empowerment and encouragement. Positive school leadership strengthens parent and family partnerships, school-wide goals, and student learning outcomes" (Johnson, 2022).

Effective school and district leaders understand that none of us can operate in a silo and expect to positively impact students and families for success. In fact, research shows that "schools, families, and communities comprise overlapping spheres that can influence student well-being, for better or worse. . . . Each is essential for student success" (Murphy, 2010; Murphy & Tobin, 2011).

As we discussed in Chapter 2, strong parent and school partnerships— where both groups work as equal partners with a shared responsibility for children's academic and social emotional development—lead to positive effects for both parents and students. Successful parent and school partnerships are "characterized by mutual trust and respect, an inclusive approach welcoming families from all backgrounds, a focus on improving students' results and success, and a process-oriented approach, in which the collaboration between schools and parents is regarded as an ongoing process which takes time, attention, and planning to sustain" (Krijnen et al., 2022). School and district leaders provide the foundation on which these partnerships can grow, resulting in a positive school climate: "an environment in which all people—not just adults or educators—are engaged and respected and where students, families, and educators work together to develop, live, and contribute to a shared school vision" (DeWitt & Slade, 2014, p. 9).

Having a positive school climate is important and can improve student achievement and the sense of belonging (Hughes & Pickeral, 2013). However, simply saying we want a positive school climate isn't enough. Neither is hoping that it will eventually happen if we "give it enough time." We have to put in the work to make it happen.

ALIGNING ACTION AND VISION

In order to reach a goal, you have to make a plan for how you're going to accomplish it. Understanding by Design principles for instructional planning follow this approach (Wiggins & McTighe, 2005)—start with the end in mind (the standard or learning outcome you want students to achieve) and then work backward to determine what student success looks like and what lessons and instruction are needed to make that happen.

We can apply similar logic to creating a school or district climate where families thrive and students achieve. In order to do that, we have to start with our vision, define what that vision looks like in practice, and then make sure that what we're actually doing is in line with what we say we want to do. As Covey (1989) would say, "Start with the end in mind".

One way to do this is through a Vision in Action analysis. In this process, you examine each of the values within your vision and write down the actions that you and the other educators in your school or district take to demonstrate those values with each other, with families and the community, and with students. The hope is that you find there are many actions that demonstrate your key values. However, you may find that there are holes where you don't demonstrate a particular value well enough or even actions that detract from that value that need to change. Or maybe you realize that the vision is just a set of words and statements that don't hold much power because it doesn't truly reflect what your school or district believes, who you are, and what you're committed to. Figure 3.1 shows a sample Vision in Action that you can adapt with your own vision and values (see also Appendix C for a Vision in Action Template).

FIGURE 3.1 Sample Vision in Action

Vision in Action

Lester Middle School

At Lester Middle School we will foster a **respectful** learning environment that builds **trust** within the community of learners to act with **integrity** and **honesty** as they gain the knowledge and skills necessary to succeed in college and careers.

VALUE	HOW DO WE DEMONSTRATE THIS VALUE WITH EACH OTHER?
Respect	• Set events and meetings at times parents can attend • Refer to parents in the manner they want to be addressed • Listen to learn and not only to respond • Be punctual by showing up on time, starting on time, and ending on time • Establish boundaries in when and how you communicate, and use appropriate last name reference
Integrity	• Establish personal code of ethics with parent/school goals and action plan • Establish norms for communicating and follow them • Be consistent • Use language to empower, speak with integrity by saying what you mean and meaning what you say • Speak with positive intentionality
Trust	• Maintain confidentiality • Maintain commitments • Follow through • Use culturally responsive and trauma-informed training
Honesty	• Be transparent • Speak using true facts and data • Demonstrate benevolence in actions: Protect the best interests of students
VALUE	HOW DO WE DEMONSTRATE THIS VALUE WITH FAMILIES AND THE COMMUNITY?
Respect	• Address parents and students by name • Acknowledge customs and traditions important to the community • Use formal communication when appropriate • Use the language necessary or give access to translators for written and spoken language
Integrity	• Maintain confidentiality • Maintain commitments • Follow through
Trust	• Establish parent/school contract or agreement to establish the interconnection and reliance between school and home

(Continued)

(Continued)

VALUE	HOW DO WE DEMONSTRATE THIS VALUE WITH FAMILIES AND THE COMMUNITY?
Honesty	• Communicate expectations clearly • Share data • Be transparent with facts

VALUE	HOW DO WE DEMONSTRATE THIS VALUE WITH STUDENTS?
Respect	• Learn family traditions • Include images of families in curriculum materials • Refer to students by name • Use systems such as Love and Logic
Integrity	• Promote an honest learning culture • Incorporate character education • Establish a grading policy promoting academic integrity • Use restorative systems
Trust	• Maintain confidentiality • Maintain commitments • Follow through • Create spaces for gathering for relationships • Build relationships and place an emphasis on students first
Honesty	• Use facts to communicate • Teach students how to communicate honestly and sincerely • Define academic dishonesty policies: cheating

Once you've completed this chart using your own vision, it's time to analyze the results. Here are some things to think about.

- **Look at each group of stakeholders.** Were any of the groups harder to complete actions for than others? For example, was it more challenging to find ways that you demonstrate each value with families and the community than with students and staff?

- **Look at each value across all stakeholder groups.** Do you equally demonstrate that value with all of the groups? Do you need to bolster commitment or brainstorm additional ways to demonstrate a particular value with all stakeholder groups?

- **Take a step back.** Reflect on the whole process. Did you find important things that you do that you couldn't assign to a particular value? Is there a missing group of stakeholders that your school or district supports? If yes, perhaps you need to revisit your vision to incorporate an additional value or more specifically address those groups of people. Conversely, did you start to realize that there are actions you or others take that actually detract from the values the vision espouses? If yes, what needs to happen in order to change those behaviors or practices?

As a result of analyzing your vision, you may realize that a variety of actions need to be set in place in order to live out the vision more fully as a school or district. Communication and accountability are key to ensuring that real change occurs, so using a tool such as the Vision in Action: Action Plan (Figure 3.2 and Appendix D) can be helpful. This template walks you through creating a goal related to the vision and then breaking it down into single action items or activities that can be done to help accomplish the goal. It also provides the opportunity to specifically think through the people and resources as well as potential funding sources you need in order to be successful.

It is also important to make sure that parents are aware of the goals in the strategic action plan and how those goals align to the school or district vision. Do not assume all parents understand what you mean when you state in your strategic plan that you plan to act with integrity or that the school will foster a climate of trust. By spelling that out and giving specific examples of what each statement means, you are building parent's social capital—understanding of behavioral norms, relational trust, and shared purpose (Torre & Murphy, 2016)—and therefore building parent's capacity to understand how they can work in partnership as educators at home. When parents and educators work together in this way, you are sharing power and responsibility for students' success beyond school and within school.

> If your school or district doesn't have a clear vision or you realize that your current vision needs some revisiting, here are some questions that can help you get started. When assembling your "vision team," make sure parents have a seat at the table too. You can't walk the talk unless everyone responsible for bringing the vision into reality is included in those conversations that build the vision.
>
> - What are your goals for your students, staff, and community?
> - What sets your school/district apart from others?
> - What values are important to your students, staff, and community?
> - What do you want your school/district to achieve?
> - What unites your school/district?

FIGURE 3.2 Vision In Action: Action Plan Template

Vision in Action

Action Plan

Goal:

KEY ACTIVITIES	BY WHOM	BY WHEN

WHAT RESOURCES DO YOU *HAVE* TO SUPPORT THE EXECUTION OF THESE ACTIONS?

WHAT RESOURCES DO YOU *NEED* TO SUPPORT THE EXECUTION OF THESE ACTIONS?

IDENTIFY ANY ADDITIONAL EXPENSES ASSOCIATED WITH THESE ACTIONS AS WELL AS POTENTIAL FUNDING SOURCES.

ASSOCIATED EXPENSE	TYPE OF EXPENSE (ONE TIME, SHORT-TERM, ONGOING)	POTENTIAL FUNDING SOURCE

WHAT ADDITIONAL SUPPORT OR OUTSIDE INVOLVEMENT DO YOU NEED TO SUPPORT THE EXECUTION OF THESE ACTIONS? (e.g., new community partner, outside consultant, district leader)

HOW WILL YOU MONITOR PROGRESS FOR EACH OF THE IDENTIFIED ACTIONS? WHAT DOES SUCCESS LOOK LIKE?

SOURCE: Adapted from Illinois and Kansas State Boards of Education School Improvement Plans.

Work Smarter, Not Harder

▶ Communication is one of the keys to building parent engagement and capacity, especially when it comes to walking the talk of your school/district vision and values. I've shared many ways that we can communicate information to parents—social media, newsletters, school marquees—but nothing beats in-person conversation. Although that may sound challenging, it's really quite simple when you maximize what you are already doing. Think about all of the in-person opportunities you have with parents at your school or district, such as daily pick up and drop off, sporting events, various meetings, and after-school programs or enrichment activities. If you know that parents are already going to be attending these events, why not maximize that opportunity by having someone stand at a table and share news and information about available programs and resources or even publicize an upcoming event. They can also answer parent questions and be an overall ambassador for your school/district. It is great if the person managing the table is a teacher or principal, but even more powerful than a school or district representative is having a parent leader represent instead. Not only is it empowering for the parent(s) who works the table but it also provides a layer of trust and authenticity to the information they are providing to their peers.

Conducting Equity Walks

As you seek to align your actions and those of your school or district with your vision, you may find that doing an equity walk through your buildings is important. An equity walk is an "observational learning walkthrough where facilitators gather and review evidence of equitable educational practices" (Hanover Research, 2020).

For the purposes of this book, consider equity walks that focus on parent engagement and community building. However, equity walks can and should also focus on other important school/district functions, such as curriculum and instruction, teacher practices, student efficacy and involvement, and school policy and organizational practices.

There are a variety of ways to conduct an equity walk, but generally the steps are as follows:

1. **Identify a specific area focus for observation.** Perhaps you need to focus on a specific aspect or practice identified through your vision work or you may decide a broader focus is necessary.

2. **Identify the observation team.** Select a team that will provide diverse perspectives and that holds a variety of roles throughout the school and the community, such as teachers, parents, administrators, local community partners, etc.

3. **Determine the walkthrough process and protocols.** During this part of the planning phase, select specific items to observe. These items should be related to the focus of the equity walk and can be divided into categories such as the physical building (hallways, bulletin boards, the library, etc.), teacher practices, and instructional routines.

4. **Conduct the equity walk.** During the equity walk, the observation team walks the school campus and records notes or information related to the selected criteria. It's important for the team to take as detailed and impartial notes as possible and to stick to observable facts, so that the subsequent analysis can be objective.

> As a school or district leader, it is important to make sure that everyone in the building understands that "equity walks are intended to gather data and evidence to facilitate discussion and reflection, rather than act as a formal evaluation of an individual's practices" (Hanover Research, 2022). Equity walks are not punitive nor are they tied to performance evaluations.

5. **Analyze, debrief, reflect, and share the results.** Once the walkthrough is complete, all observations should be compiled and analyzed. The purpose is to find trends, strengths, and areas of improvement. Once evidence is analyzed and reflected on, key findings and results should be shared with all stakeholders. Agreed on action items should then become part of the school or district strategic action plan in order to communicate the changes and hold necessary stakeholders or implementers accountable.

Figure 3.3 offers suggestions of things to consider in order to conduct an equity walk with a focus on parent engagement and building capacity.

FIGURE 3.3 Things to Look for During an Equity Walk

	THINGS TO LOOK FOR DURING AN EQUITY WALK . . .
Building Environment	• Welcoming signage inside and out invites parents in and shares information about how to properly check in at the office and navigate the building • Culturally responsive images on the walls are reflective of cultures and races of children who attend the school and indicate a sense of belonging to students and parents • Bulletin boards and displayed student work reflect strong academic focus and clearly demonstrate to parents what is being learned in class • Information on how to become involved in upcoming events, workshops, volunteer opportunities, etc. is posted and available • There are areas specifically designated to house resources for parents and for them to convene, participate, and learn throughout the school building
Interactions With Parents	• Friendly staff welcome parents when they drop off and pick up students on campus • Parent questions, feedback, and suggestions are welcomed and solicited • Front office staff are welcoming, prioritize visitors, and provide clear information as needed • A translator is available when needed and access to translators is clear • Feedback and questions are welcomed (evidenced by the presence of a box for written notes, a poster with a QR code to digitally submit, etc.)
Diversity and Cultural Responsiveness	• Images, posters, etc. on the walls are reflective of cultures and races of students who attend the school • Culturally responsive communication is apparent and information is translated into other languages used within the school • Instructional materials and resources reflect the diversity of the students who attend the school • Activities and events honor the cultures reflected at the school

THREE KEYS TO WALKING THE TALK

In addition to aligning your vision and actions, there are three key principles to walk the talk to build parent capacity and engagement.

• Seek to understand in order to serve

• Seek to remove barriers

• Seek to build efficacy

Seek to Understand in Order to Serve

In *The 7 Habits of Highly Effective People* (1989) Stephen Covey introduced the idea of "seek first to understand, then to be understood." This habit is all about listening to truly understand what a person is saying rather than listening with the intent to reply. Another way to think about this is the difference simply between being listened to versus being heard. Both involve the act of someone listening to what you have to say, but being heard implies that the listener also understands the significance of what you're saying and then does something with that understanding.

Listening Tours

Good leaders listen first. They listen in order to learn, to understand, to make connections, and to build relationships. They listen in order to seek alternative perspectives and to amplify others' voices.

The use of listening tours—my sneaker philosophy—is a simple but effective tool to use to figure out where/what the needs are in the community. The more often school leaders are out in the community meeting parents where they are at, instead of expecting parents to come to them, the more empowered parents will become to share their voice.

Listening tours can be formal or informal, as well as advertised or unannounced, depending on the type of information you are hoping to gather. By going out into the community to speak with families and community members, you are showing people that their voice matters and that you are willing to do the work of going to them rather than requiring them to come to you.

Formal listening tours: Formal listening tours typically have a specific focus as well as prearranged and advertised meeting opportunities. For example, if the focus of a listening tour is about understanding student and family health you may arrange a meeting or a coffee forum of leaders from local clinics and medical and dental facilities to share their experiences and perspectives. You may also schedule visits to local health care facilities to better understand those physical building conditions and the experiences of the people who use them (e.g., wait times, access to prescriptions, cleanliness). You may then schedule a series of porch visits to talk to parents about their experiences in obtaining medical and dental services—what they like, what challenges or barriers they have, and what they wish could be different.

Meet Them Where They Are

▶ If you are just starting to be visible within the community, it may take some time for families to be accepting of school leaders or other educators showing up at their homes. Some families may only have experience with social service agencies or law enforcement visiting their homes and may be reluctant to meet at first. Immigrant families, especially those with language barriers, may not understand the purpose for the visit.

I have found that the idea of a "porch visit" is often more approachable to parents than a "home visit." Parents may not feel confident or comfortable inviting an educator into their home but often have no problem speaking with them on the front porch, the deck, or elsewhere outside their home. In fact, parents typically welcome someone from the school taking time to come to them instead of requesting that they come to the school. One way to further remove reluctance around home or porch visits is to schedule them in advance, making sure to share the purpose, time commitment, structure, and participants. This will help set an expectation for the visit and can ease any uncertainty parents may have.

In Topeka, we like to bring small, personalized gift baskets to these visits. We do our best to make sure that the items we bring (e.g., books, learning games, baby bottles, snacks, pamphlets about specific community and school resources) are useful and meaningful to the family and help build a relationship with them.

If the parent wasn't home or did not answer the door for some reason, leaving behind a "We Stopped By" door hanger message can be especially effective in helping reschedule the visit. On the door hanger, you can leave a handwritten message outlining the purpose of the visit and a contact number. For parents who may not read English, make sure to include a number they can call for translation support.

Informal listening tours: Informal listening tours may have a specific focus, but the qualitative data gathering is much more relaxed than in a formal listening tour. You may have some preplanned questions to use to start a conversation, but you let the conversation flow organically. As a school leader, your physical presence out in the community is nearly as important as the information that community members choose to share with you. Often people are more willing to speak freely about the questions and topics you bring up because they are in their community setting (e.g., a football game or a laundromat), rather than a more formal school setting.

Here are some ideas of places to go:

- Youth sporting events
- Local churches
- Popular community restaurants
- Laundromats
- Grocery stores
- Neighborhoods and parks
- Community centers

Ultimately, the more we seek to understand and truly listen to the needs, fears, challenges, and barriers that exist for parents and families, the more ownership we can take in removing those barriers—it's not about parents conforming to the norms of school and figuring out how they fit into what we are doing—it's about us adapting how we approach parent engagement and the role of the school as the center of the community so that both families and students can be successful (Auerbach, 2010).

Parent Surveys

Another way to seek information from parents is through the use of surveys. This provides parents the opportunity to share feedback, questions, and comments about the school or district across a variety of topics, including information about themselves, their students, the school atmosphere, barriers to engagement, and community needs.

When conducting surveys, it is important to consider how to distribute them and what methods you will use to gather the information. You might provide hard copies with return drop boxes or have QR codes posted at popular locations (churches, restaurants, stores) throughout the community. Determine whether your parents will be responsive to a text of the survey so that they can respond on their phones rather than needing a Wi-Fi connection on a computer. Remember to offer the survey in a variety of languages and include your American Sign Language community to encourage all parents to respond and to remove any language barriers that might exist. Figure 3.4 offers some guidance for crafting parent surveys.

FIGURE 3.4 Ideas for Effective Parent Surveys

1. **Begin with a broad question to investigate.** Here are some ideas:
   - How well is your school bridging racial, class, and cultural differences?
   - How does communication function at your school?
   - How well does your school support parent and community engagement?
   - How welcoming is your school?
   - How does your school share power and practice democracy?
   - In what ways does your school support students for academic success?

2. **Develop a set of detailed statements** that specifically address the broader question as well as a rating system to respond to the statements. Here is an example of a broad question and three detailed statements:
   - How does communication function at your school?
     - Communication from administrators is clear and timely.
     - Communication from my child's teachers is clear and timely.
     - Communication is translated into a language I can read at home.
     - I only hear from the school when there is a problem.
   - Here are some suggestions for rating scales:
     - always, often, something, rarely, never
     - already doing this, could do this easily, this will take time, this will be hard
     - strongly agree, somewhat agree, agree, somewhat disagree, strongly disagree

3. **Decide on a strategy and timeline for distributing and collecting the surveys.** Make sure to consider alternative and flexible approaches to distribution and in gathering, as suggested at the outset of this section.

4. **Gather and analyze the data and make an action plan as a result of what you learn.**

LIVED AND LEARNED

Prioritize and Tackle What You Can With Impact

▶ Following the pandemic, many needs surfaced as a result of the listening tours and parent surveys we conducted throughout our Topeka communities. The needs felt overwhelming at times. One of the greatest needs we identified from the feedback was for educational opportunities for two-year-olds after we placed preschools for three- and four-year-olds in almost every school, but did not originally have funding in place for two-year-olds. We knew we could tackle this high priority area with the help of others. Our administrator for early childhood brainstormed resources and through continued collaboration with the school community and administrators providing oversight for early childhood, we received a grant from the Topeka Community Foundation, who was a participant of impact investing in the social determinants of health. We piloted our first two-year-old early childhood program within an existing preschool during the 2022–2023 school year, and it became self-sustainable as the year ended, as a result of proper licensing implementation and qualification for state funding opportunities. We were also able to offer a reduced tuition rate for staff. Due to the creativity of staff and parents, and amplifying the voices of a team who collectively are more resourceful than any single leader, the program has become a recruitment tool for staff and is a tremendous resource for all parents.

Seek to Remove Barriers

It is important to determine what types of issues or challenges keep parents from coming to the school and being engaged in the school. I often ask parents the questions, "What gets in the way of being connected to the school?" and "What can be done differently to increase parental engagement?" I have learned a lot from these questions. Often it's food, shelter, transportation, parenting support, and Maslow's basic needs. Responses from these questions can help you identify clear pathways to build parent capacity so that parents can become connected and see themselves as part of the school.

The purpose of removing barriers to parent engagement is to empower families to help their children academically and socially, to connect parents with each other and with the community, and to offer resources to support families with their overall health and success. Ultimately, the capacity of parents increases when we build bridges between their needs and services within the school community, allowing them to view the school as an extension of their community.

Studies have found that once barriers are identified, parents and school staff may offer contrasting solutions. "While parent solutions directly address the barriers identified and support parent engagement, staff frequently offered disconnected solutions, reiterating parent involvement—the necessity of parents being present in the building, rather than parent engagement" (Baker et al., 2016). Thus, once barriers are identified—through listening tours, parent surveys, etc.—it is also important to engage parents in finding solutions for those barriers. They must be the ones to answer the question posed earlier in this chapter: "What can be done differently to increase parental engagement?" Figure 3.5 lists some creative solutions that have worked in schools across the country. (Chapter 4 will focus more on how to establish partnerships to remove identified barriers, build parent capacity, and improve student outcomes.)

FIGURE 3.5   Barriers to Parent Engagement and Solutions

BARRIER	POTENTIAL SOLUTION
Limited access to fresh produce or groceries	Create a community garden and provide opportunity for students and families to plant and maintain the garden. At harvest, food is sent home with students who need it most; offer food pantries on campus stocked through partnership with the local food bank or through corporate and church donations
Unsafe activity occurring in neighborhoods	Hold community conversations with the police department and work together to create neighborhood watch organizations
Limited or unsafe access to laundry facilities	Place a washer and dryer at the school and allow parents to use it in exchange for volunteer hours at the school

BARRIER	POTENTIAL SOLUTION
Limited access to health services	Partner with local clinics to provide mobile dental, medical, and mental health services on school campus on a regular basis
Unreliable access to transportation for school conferences	Use virtual meeting technology to eliminate the need for families to come on campus; partner with city transportation services to offer discounted rates when used specifically for school-related transportation; schedule conferences somewhere out in the community that is more accessible for specific groups of families, such as at a church or the local homeless shelter
Unstable employment	Work diligently to hire parents in your community for open positions within the school or district, such as cafeteria staff, paraprofessional positions, campus security, janitorial staff, and more; create a parent leadership cohort and provide them with the necessary training to receive compensation for in-demand services or support they then offer to the school, such as tutoring, administrative services, after-school programming implementation, etc.
Lack of childcare after school	Partner with a local community-based organization to begin offering free after-school programming, including homework support and enrichment opportunities; parents who enroll must sign a contract committing to a specific number of volunteer hours per school year as well as attendance at a certain number of parent capacity-building workshops per year

LIVED AND LEARNED

Use What You've Got

▶ When I first began in Topeka, one of our incredible speech pathologists Peggy Fisher shared that very few parents were bringing in their preschool-aged children to receive the speech services they qualified for. She was concerned because she knew the children across the county desperately needed the services in order to be ready for kindergarten.

So, I met with the speech pathologists to discuss the issue and they shared similar concerns. Essentially, the free early intervention services to address and correct speech issues were not being accessed by all parents, causing some students to begin school with delayed speech issues that could have been corrected while language skills were forming. This also meant that older elementary students who could have also benefited from the services as a supplemental support beyond the school day, did not receive extra support that could have reduced how fast they improved in speech and language, ultimately impacting their reading and literacy development. As a group, the speech pathologists strongly felt that just because parents were not coming to the school for services did not mean they did not need or want the services for their children. So, Fisher led the charge and decided that we had to change the way we provided the service, by going to families instead of requiring families to come to us.

(Continued)

(Continued)

In thinking through ways to bring the services to the students, Fisher and her husband, an elementary science teacher in the district, asked if they could use a resource we already had—a maintenance van in limited use in the district maintenance lot. They asked if they could repurpose it with a little paint and some changes to the interior, and, of course, we said yes! With the help of their colleagues in the maintenance service department, they painted the exterior with a rainbow of bright polka dots and renovated the interior to include toddler-sized table space and all the activities and resources needed to provide mobile speech and language services inside the van. They decided to call it the Tot SPOT, with the acronym SPOT standing for **S**peech, **P**hysical therapy, and **O**ccupational therapy **T**eachers. As soon as it was ready, Fisher and her staff began driving it all over Topeka to bring those vital services to families and remove the transportation barrier that so many parents were experiencing. This one out-of-the-box step increased access to speech and helped improve literacy rates that year. In 2017, the Tot SPOT was recognized nationally with a Magna award from the National School Board Association, thereby allowing other districts to replicate the van concept with various other mobile services. Ask yourself if there are underutilized resources you already have that if repurposed could have an even larger impact.

Removing the Communication Barrier

Communication is often cited as a barrier to parent engagement in school. When this is the case, challenges in communication often center on aspects of the following:

- **Timeliness:** Is information shared with enough notice (or even shared at all) for parents to act on it or respond adequately? Is communication proactive and positive instead of reactive and sent only after problems with behavior or academics arise?

- **Quality:** Is the communication meaningful and respectful? Does the communication provide value to parents?

- **Clarity:** Is the communication clear in purpose and does it provide complete and correct information?

- **Regularity:** Is communication sent according to a mutually understood schedule and through understood methods (email, text, print, app) so that parents know what to expect and where to look for information? Does communication occur frequently enough that parents feel connected to and informed about the school?

- **Translation:** Is communication translated into parents' home languages so they are able to access the information in the same way that native English speakers can?

Much like with educators and leaders, communication is foundational to building parent capacity. DeWitt (2017) found that schools typically communicate in four different ways, which often reflect the school leader's communication style.

1. **Collaborative communication:** We build collective efficacy together. We have parent representatives on our committees and seek input from parents to inform our communication.

2. **Negotiation communication:** We care what you say but want you to agree with us.

3. **Regulation communication:** This is what you need to know and that's it.

4. **Bystander communication:** We will wait to have an issue before we communicate with you.

While I can rationalize the occasional situational need for each of those types of communication approaches, ultimately the most effective method is collaboration, where communication builds collective efficacy, is grounded in community norms and cultural responsiveness, and reinforces the notion that involvement of families is highly valued (Hoover-Dempsey, Walker, Sandler, Whetsel et al., 2005; Leo et al., 2019; Lewis et al., 2011).

As a school or district leader, in order to improve communication between educators and parents you must understand both groups' perspectives and perceptions. Consider conducting a listening tour or administering a survey with each group. Once you have feedback from both groups, you will better know what to work on or how to improve.

Seek to Build Efficacy

Have you ever read *The Little Engine That Could* (1930)? It's the story of a small train engine determined to get over a seemingly insurmountable mountain. With confidence and determination, the little engine repeats the words, "I-think-I-can, I-think-I-can," all the way to the top, and delights in his success when he reaches his goal and goes down the other side of the mountain. *The Little Engine That Could* is a model of self-efficacy.

Researchers have found three key factors that affect whether parents are motivated to become engaged in their children's learning (Hoover-Dempsey, Walker, & Sandler, 2005):

1. How parents develop their roles/job descriptions as parents: Do they understand school expectations and what school is asking of them? What do their friends and family think is acceptable?

2. How confident parents feel about their ability to help their children: Do they feel they have the knowledge and skills to make a difference?

3. Whether they feel invited, both by their children and the school: Do they get strong, positive signals from teachers and students that they should be involved?

Underlying each of these factors are beliefs of self-efficacy, "people's beliefs about their capabilities to produce designated levels of performance that exercise influence over events and affect their lives. Self-efficacy beliefs determine how people feel, think, motivate themselves, and behave" (Bandura, 1994, p. 2). Self-efficacy is important for everyone in the school community—leaders, parents, educators, and students—and is key to building collective success and improving student and parent outcomes. And as we think about concrete ways to engage parents in school and their children's educational lives, it's important to understand how capacity and efficacy are intertwined not only for families but for teachers as well.

Figure 3.6 illustrates a model of capacity and efficacy for growth and success. As parent capacity is built (by removing barriers to engagement, providing helpful classes and workshops, sharing power and amplifying parent voice, etc.) their self-efficacy increases, and they feel more in control and confident to engage in partnership with their child's teacher and support their child academically and socially. As this happens, teacher capacity increases—teachers understand their students better and can increase their skills and abilities to teach them effectively. And as teacher capacity increases, their self-efficacy increases, and they feel more impactful with their instruction and their ability to increase student achievement and to work in partnership with parents. It is a continuous learning cycle. The more capacity grows, the more efficacy grows, which leads to more capacity and more efficacy, ultimately resulting in improved outcomes for students and the lived experience of the power of collective efficacy.

FIGURE 3.6 A Model of Capacity and Efficacy for Growth and Success

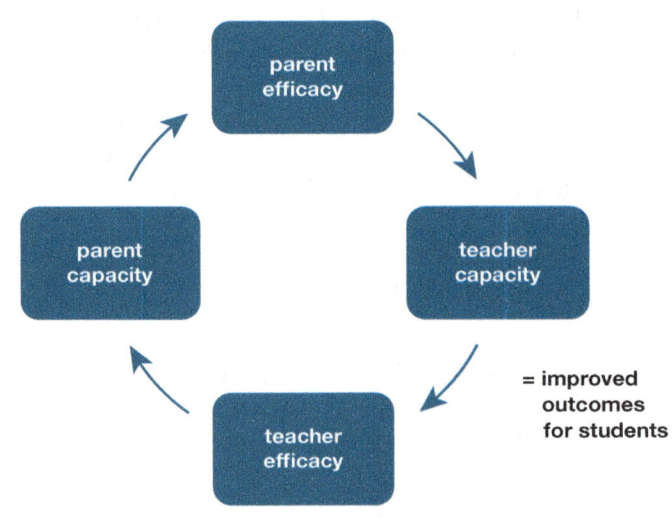

BUILDING PARENT CAPACITY IN HIGH-POVERTY SCHOOLS

You Can't Give What You Don't Have

▶ As a school and district leader for more than twenty-five years, I know from personal experience how challenging it can be to walk the talk. It's important to keep in mind that you can't give what you don't have. So, one way to build efficacy and capacity in other people is to build efficacy and capacity in yourself. Then, you're able to authentically model and live that out. And the more you can allow for your life experiences and the lessons you've learned to be part of the story that you share with parents (and other educators), the more impactful and authentic you are as a leader and a guide to families.

Let's practice this right now. Open up your calendar with the intentionality of prioritizing how you use time. If you're like me, if it's not scheduled in my calendar, it's not happening. So, look at your schedule for the next two weeks. Where have you planned time for yourself? Where have you planned time with your family and friends? If you have young children, this is not about just attending their basketball game or piano recital. It's about real time to be their parent. It is important to prioritize the people and connections within your life as part of your routine to intentionally walk the talk in your own life.

Part of building parents' self-efficacy is giving them tools they need to be successful in engaging with schools. Historically, schools are built on white, middle-class norms for behavior. The parents who we serve in our schools come from a variety of cultural and linguistic backgrounds, socioeconomic levels, and lived experiences and may not understand those norms and behaviors or may have a different definition of what those norms and behaviors look like in practice. This is why it is important to integrate culturally relevant literature and resources to expand the knowledge base of everyone being served and integrate character-based lessons that also show the many ways students and parents may use language and behavior to convey character traits such as integrity, respect, and responsibilty to thrive in any circumstance regardless of their socioeconomic background. Those educational opportunities can be used to help parents understand how to model the behaviors with their children at home and how those behaviors benefit their children both inside and outside of the classroom, which can lead to future success.

For example, let's look at the character trait of responsibility. When working with parents, it is important to clearly define the idea of responsibility as well as provide concrete examples and behavioral practices. Responsibility is not only turning homework in on time or studying for a test, but it's also about being prepared with all materials when students come to class/school.

It can also be reflected in a child's attendance rate. Helping parents see their role in getting their child to school on time and equating school to their child's practice place for the real world of work can help reduce chronic absenteeism. It is eye opening for parents to learn that if their child misses just two days a month, over the course of the school year that actually equates to eighteen total school days. This absence rate can lead to poor academic performance, their child's potential inability to learn to read, and even increase the likelihood their child will eventually drop out of school (Attendance Works, 2018). By focusing on character and intentionally bringing parents into the learning and discussion, we open the door to wider possibilities of change and care in the community.

Two organizations that support character development and capacity building for parents and students are Parents as Teachers (parentsasteachers.org) and National Schools of Character (character.org). Schools can apply for grants to bring this programming to their areas.

Another aspect of character building is how to help build parent capacity around effective ways to handle conflict and imbalances of power and promote restorative practices. By offering workshops, training, and information to parents on these topics, we help parents learn productive ways to challenge discriminatory attitudes and behaviors, how to promote asset-based language and empathy, how to constructively advocate for themselves and their children, and how to hold each other and the school accountable to work collectively for the success of all students.

Depending on the needs of the community and the school climate as partnerships begin to take root, the use of restorative circles may help build or repair trust, create community, and promote constructive problem solving. Although typically associated with restorative classroom work among students in an educational setting, restorative circles can be used among adults as well. In a parent-school partnership context, there are three major purposes of restorative circles:

- Contribute to a positive school culture that values parent voice and choice and ensures learning

- Assist parents in working through issues and situations that affect their self-efficacy and their engagement with and participation in school, whether directly or indirectly

- Build the capacity of the parent and school community to communicate respectfully, arrive at a consensus, make decisions, and take action (adapted from Fisher & Frey, 2022)

As parents build relationships among each other through restorative circles and other efficacy and capacity-building experiences, they gain the tools to act collectively and potentially more powerfully as school and community leaders to effect change (Delgado-Gaitan, 2001; Warren et al., 2009). "Strong relationships among parents create mutual support and a sense of community out of which parents can develop as leaders, and the assertion of their leadership can produce change in power relationships and the culture of schooling" (Warren et al., 2009, p. 239).

FOLLOW THROUGH WITH URGENCY AND TRANSPARENCY

The ultimate display of walking the talk for a school or district leader is following through with commitments and action plans with urgency and transparency. When collecting and analyzing data from formal surveys, listening tours, a parent advisory committee, or a parent feedback form, it is important parents know what is being collected, how it is being used, and how they can obtain access to any collected data about their student and their school. Parents should have simple and immediate access to view accountability in the action steps being taken, which demonstrates importance, establishes trust, and shows commitment to following through.

As improvements are implemented from parent feedback, it is important for parents to know the outcomes and what improvements were made. This creates a culture of responsiveness at the school/district. Social media can be a powerful tool for this, as well. Parents will feel more empowered and will be more likely to share their voice again when they see the impact that they can have and the changes that can be made as a result. As the school focuses on improvement goals such as chronic absenteeism, posting the attendance rate outside of classrooms, on the marquee, and in the school online and print newsletters can help engage parents by sharing information publicly. As parents share suggestions, feedback portals such as blogs, social media sites, and discussion forums in person or electronically can be used to have interactive communication. Direct communication with families at athletic or other extracurricular events can also be effective, such as at a table or booth.

With Listening Comes the Responsibility to Act

▶ I was superintendent of Jennings School District during the time that Michael Brown was murdered in the neighboring city of Ferguson, Missouri. It was a challenging time because we had families and students who either knew or were relatives of the Brown family or were impacted by the unrest that occurred as a result of his death. As a district it was important that we met them with compassion and understanding, using a trauma-informed approach for our staff, families, and students who needed counseling, health services, or other partners in the community to address critical needs.

During the time in which school walkouts were occurring nationally, we learned through word of mouth and social media that our high school students were planning a walkout too. As students picked up their backpacks to walk out of the building, we commanded their attention and asked them what their goals were in walking out. They weren't sure, but they knew it was the right thing to do. Therefore, as educators and advocates for our students, we decided to walk alongside them so that they understood through our actions that we were with them and heard their voices. Amid our shouts of, "No Justice, No Peace," I realized that in order to help the students learn how to use their voices effectively, we needed to teach them how to do more than just march. So we got the students together and urged them to make a list of three things they wanted to change and bring it to school with them the next day. At the start of first period across the entire school, every teacher spent the first part of class allowing students to share their lists and then compiled them into a collective school list. As a result of those conversations, three common demands arose: body cameras, community policing, and more Black Americans on the police force.

With those three demands in hand, we told the students we would get a bus, and before school started on Friday, we would take it halfway to the Jennings police station and then march together the rest of the way down the street to share our list with the police. What we wanted the students to understand was that in order to use their power, they have to be educated and prepared to use their voice effectively. And anyone who tells them to skip school to march may be missing the bigger picture, stressing the importance of education. And so, we did just that.

After talking with the police department, they agreed to all our demands, and we saw quick action, including the appointment of Black school police resource officers in the school district. Ultimately, what this experience showed our community was that if you put people first and you listen and give them a voice, amazing and sustainable transformation can take place.

WALKING THE TALK IN ACTION

I first met Dr. Nick Gardner when he was a physical education teacher at Quincy Elementary. He served as a teacher in Topeka Public Schools for many years and was making the transition to school leadership. His father, Cleo Gardner, had been a school principal for many years and a model of what walking the talk looks like in action within the community of Topeka. Nick had always looked up to his father's leadership example.

As a result of watching his father over the years, coupled with encounters he had with students, Nick understood the importance of being a positive role model for his students and an advocate for families. Nick was placed as an administrator intern at Eisenhower Middle School to build his leadership capacity and make connections in order to eventually lead at Ross, the connecting elementary school. When he was hired at Ross in the summer of 2022, he spent the weeks leading up to the first day of school meeting with groups and attending events in southeast Topeka in order to better get to know the community. I became Nick's mentor for his doctoral research, which he was working on during that same time period.

Nick's approach aligned with the district approach. And when he started as principal during the 2022–2023 school year, he worked to involve the community in visible ways at his school. This included employing at least 10 percent of the school's staff from the surrounding neighborhood and bringing to Ross the adult-student mentorship program he started called Inspired Minds. He works tirelessly to achieve those goals, empowering those around him to help make Ross Elementary the best that it can be.

Nick earned his doctorate during his first year as principal, showing the other Black male students who look up to him a model of excellence in education. "It creates a sense of belief," he said. "It's a job, but I also see it as a responsibility, not only to help make Ross the best school in Topeka, but to open doors for these students" (Garcia, 2022). Nick understands the important role he plays in promoting positive behavior supports throughout his school, disrupting the potential school-to-prison pipeline so common for children of color. His approach seeks to break stereotypes, inspire engagement in parents and students, and empower the community to share its own narrative. As a result, parent engagement, partnerships, and volunteerism increased tremendously his first year, drastically improving the school and community culture. Hundreds of parents and community volunteers gave their time, talent, and resources in support of Dr. Gardner's vision of building parent, teacher, and student capacity. Dr. Gardner not only walks the talk, but also teaches others to walk alongside him to carry out the vision they collaboratively created as a school community.

WALKING THE TALK REFLECTION

Think back to what you read throughout this chapter. Use these reflection questions to consider your own school or district and the role you play in building parent capacity.

1. What does it mean to you to walk the talk? How do you currently walk the talk in your school or district?

2. In what ways do you currently "seek to understand"? What, if anything, would you like to improve in that area?

3. Which communication type is reflected within your district, school, or classroom: collaborative, negotiation, regulation, or bystander? Why do you think it is that way?

4. Think about the relationship between parent capacity and efficacy and teacher capacity and efficacy. As an educational leader your self-efficacy is important too. What can you do to build your own self-efficacy?

Take some time to reflect on your learning and action plan your next steps.

WHAT?

Summarize your learning and key takeaways from this chapter.

SO WHAT?

Record ideas about how your key takeaways apply to you, your school, and/or your district.

NOW WHAT?

Based on your key takeaways, plan your next steps for moving forward in this area.

CHAPTER 4

Building Capacity Through Powerful Partnerships

"Coming together is a beginning, staying together is progress, and working together is success."

—attributed to Henry Ford (1863–1947)

School and district leaders have a long list of responsibilities, ranging from budgeting, to staffing, to meeting many diverse academic needs. Prioritizing according to your vision and mission and being strategic with your time and resources is critical to ensuring short- and long-range strategic goals are met. In *The 7 Habits of Highly Effective People*, Covey (1989) writes, "The key is not to prioritize what's on your schedule, but to schedule your priorities. Most of us spend too much time on what is urgent and not enough time on what is important."

As I shared in Chapter 3, aligning your leadership practices and the practices of the school/district to your vision is key to walking the talk. But no matter how much energy, creativity, and strategic planning you bring to your role, you can't build parent capacity alone. The collective energy from those who are invested in the community and who depend on the success of the school is critical to building the capacity of parents. You need the perspective, feedback, and support of school/district staff, teachers, parents, and community organizations in order to effect positive change, remove barriers, and meet the needs of the families you serve. The collective efficacy of the members that make up the school community will transform the community as they see themselves as vital to the health and success of the organization.

As you seek to address the needs of the families and students in your school and district and engage the community, it is important to avoid purchasing programs that will come and go with the budget, the leader, or the vision, and instead focus on systems that will continue to work into the future.

Some steps to start the process that have worked well for me include:

1. **Make a list of the services and needs** identified through parent surveys, discussions with parent advisory groups, etc. (Chapter 3 contains more information about gathering information about community needs.)

2. **Decide which services and needs should be top priority.** Although it may sound appealing and exciting to provide mobile dentistry services to all the schools in your district, if families already have access to dental clinics in your area, then you aren't really addressing a need. Parents will feel more understood when you actually offer services they *need* as opposed to offering services that *you* want to offer or that duplicate things already available. You can evaluate the list of needs/services using questions, such as:

   - Which needs are cited most often?

   - Which services would support the largest population of families?

   - Which services would have the greatest impact on students' academic readiness, physical well-being, or mental well-being?

   - Which services would develop the capacity of parents to be more engaged at school (e.g., addressing needs such as family financial literacy, academics, managing their child's behavior, parenting skills, mental health, or housing)?

   - What do the data in your community tell you about existing and unmet needs and services?

   - How can you incorporate the services/needs within your school as the center of the community in building the capacity of parents in support of students?

3. **Research businesses or organizations that can address those top priority needs/services.** When doing this research, consider both local and national organizations, and don't be afraid to think outside the box. For example, when I worked in Jennings School District, we realized there was a lack of laundromats and housing facilities that offer laundry services. Parents voiced this need, and so we contacted the washing machine manufacturers we felt could help. Supporters agreed to donate laundry-washing materials. In exchange for one hour of classroom volunteering, parents could come and do a load of laundry at the school. It was a win-win for all of us! The parents were able to provide clean clothes for their families free of charge, and we got the benefit of having more parents on campus supporting our students and teachers.

4. **Schedule time to brainstorm and discuss potential partnership ideas with identified businesses and organizations.** When brainstorming potential partnership ideas, it is important to reflect on ways in which your school/district can provide benefit or value to the partnership as part of a mutually beneficial relationship. For example, if you're pursuing a partnership with local businesses to conduct a quarterly job fair at one of your high school campuses, collaboratively plan based on unmet labor market needs in the community and collaboratively plan the location, focusing on things such as:

    *   Free venue that allows the business to recruit and the school to provide candidates
    *   Potential for high attendance of both adults and eligible high school aged workers
    *   Economic benefit of decreasing unemployment within the community
    *   Economic value of recycling dollars within the community—the more people locally employed, the more money they have to spend at local businesses

    When businesses and philanthropic organizations understand the relationship that directly and indirectly impacts their business community, they are more likely to contribute support in some manner. Proactively as part of the system of building capacity, it is important leaders provide information about the interconnected nature between schools and the community organization. The family—the parent, the child—we help now, ultimately becomes the individual that is the neighbor, the employee, and the resident in the community that will impact the community later. Helping businesses see the return on their investment through successful students and parents who are members of their organization or who live near their organization can help the business community see the direct correlation between their investment and outcomes in schools. Another way to demonstrate direct and indirect impact with businesses can be to discuss economic dollars. Do you (business leader) want to live in a community where you are recycling economic dollars and investing in the people who live there? We all benefit when people are employed and are positively contributing to the economic health of our city. If you want that, then it's a good idea to invest in what we're sharing.

5. **Assemble a qualified team to execute and maintain the partnership.** As a school leader, you only have so much capacity to generate, execute, and maintain any new program, let alone myriad community-school partnerships. Once a partnership or new program has been identified and planned, assembling a qualified team can help ensure that the partnership lasts over many years and can sustain itself even through staff turnover.

Seek Information From
Multiple Sources and Perspectives

▶ When I first started as the superintendent of Topeka Public Schools, I sent about 100 invitations to local businesses, agencies, and organizations for a meet and greet. People were interested in who I was, as the first Black woman superintendent in Topeka Public Schools, and I wanted to learn more about their organizations and the needs of the community. So, I set up the event at the highest poverty high school in our district, and many local leaders showed up. At the event, I asked them this question: What are the barriers that get in the way of families being able to interact with their children, become engaged in schools, and stay connected to the community in a healthy way? Here were some of their responses:

- Affordable on-site childcare for infants and toddlers so that families could attend meetings or events at school

- Availability and accessibility of fresh produce due to limited grocery options

- Limited hours of public transportation; public transit system ends at 6:00 p.m., limiting the opportunity to attend evening events or meetings at school

- Language barriers preventing families from participating or understanding available resources (at the time, the school district did not have a web page that translated content and in-person translation services were very limited)

Of course, each group had a different perspective based on their function or niche in the community, but it was a great way for me to hear what they felt the needs and barriers were and begin to identify potential partners to connect with down the road.

PARTNERSHIPS TO REMOVE
BARRIERS AND BUILD CAPACITY

Although removing barriers for parent engagement and building capacity will look different in every school and every district, some common community needs and potential partnership ideas include partners who will assist in supporting the social determinants of health, which include "the conditions in the environments where people are born, live, learn, work, play, worship, and age that affect a wide range of health, functioning, and quality-of-life outcomes and risks" (US Department of Health and Human Services, 2024).

The social determinants of health are divided into five domains: economic stability, education access and quality, health care access and quality, neighborhood and built environment, and social and community context.

Public health partnerships are often not used but they are often the most willing to partner because they understand the important role of schools and parents within the context of the social determinants of health, particularly in low-income families where infant mortality rates are higher, food deserts are more common, and health disparities are significant. Examples of partnership teams I have worked alongside are provided here as a starting place from which to build.

Digital Divide: Wi-Fi Access and Connectivity

Although the acute challenges of internet access for full-time remote access and hybrid learning due to the COVID-19 pandemic are seemingly in our past, according to the National Center for Education Statistics (NCES), 4.4 million students do not have access to computers at home, and 3.7 million don't have internet access at home (USA Facts, 2020). Given the tremendous reliance on connectivity for community resources, including telehealth, school, electronic library card use when the library is too far, grocery access when transportation to stores is limited, etc., lack of connectivity further widens the resource gap for parents. Partnering with your state's Department of Commerce to provide access and connectivity to families is a first step, and it can lead to access to resources that include:

- **Affordable Connectivity Program:** This is a federally funded program that provides a $30 discount on monthly internet bills for qualifying households (Federal Communications Commission, 2024). Among the qualifications, families whose children are enrolled for free or reduced lunch can receive the benefit. Unfortunately, only about 25 percent of eligible households that qualify are even enrolled. A resource for school districts called the Affordable Connectivity Program Adoption Toolkit can be found at EducationSuperHighway.org.

- **T-Mobile Project 10Million:** This program is run in partnership with Boys and Girls Club of America and T-Mobile, and is committed to connecting students in Grades K–12 with Wi-Fi and data. Families, schools, or entire districts can apply. Each qualifying household receives a free hotspot with 100GB of data per year for five years.

- **MobileCitizen.org:** This nonprofit provides low-cost mobile internet with unlimited data plans exclusively to

> "Ensuring that books are available to any child at any time of the year will be a good first step in enhancing the reading achievement of low-income students and an absolutely necessary step in closing the reading achievement gap."
>
> —Allington and McGill-Franzen (2009)

nonprofit organizations, educational entities, libraries, and social welfare agencies. Through partnership with this organization and coordination with other qualifying agencies in your community, you could bring internet access to students and their families throughout many locations in your community.

Local Library and Literacy Resources

There are more than 160 million people across the United States without a library card (Rowe, 2018). Libraries offer more than just books. They provide internet and computer access, access to digital content (books, magazines, podcasts, etc.), printing services, and even limited tech support. There are also many programs available to support things like adult/child literacy development, job searching, mental and physical health, and cultural awareness/celebration. In order to provide easier access to library resources, especially for those who do not have a state-issued ID, public libraries now offer digital library cards (Instant Digital Cards). This library card can be applied for online and only requires a valid mobile number. Digital access to online content is then available instantly. However, this type of service isn't the only way to take advantage of partnerships with local or county libraries. Here is another example: In Topeka Public Schools, the local library and our staff realized that many students and families were not taking advantage of the services and resources available at the public libraries. To eliminate this access barrier, we worked to create a partnership with the Topeka and Shawnee County Public Library system, where families are able to opt-in for a free library card when enrolling their children online or in-person. This empowers parents by providing them access to all physical items at every branch/bookmobile that is part of the county library system as well all of their online databases, e-books, digital audiobooks, and streaming videos.

In addition to increasing access to free resources in the library, providing greater access to books remains important for parents to ensure children have print-rich materials at home as an extension of the classroom. Research shows that children in low-income families have access to fewer reading materials than children of middle- and upper-income families (Krashen et al., 2012; Lindsay, 2010). However, the most successful way to improve the reading achievement of low-income children is to increase their access to print. Communities ranking higher on assessment measures have several factors in common: an abundance of books in public libraries, easy access to books in the community at large, and a large number of textbooks per student (Neuman & Celano, 2001). Here are some resources to support students' access to books:

- **First Book Marketplace** is a website where educators can shop for new books at steep discounts—typically 50 percent to 90 percent off. To qualify, the school must have a student population where 70 percent or more qualify for free or reduced lunch.

- **KidsNeedtoRead.org** provides books, periodicals, and literacy resources to schools, libraries, and other organizations that administer literacy programs to disadvantaged children and adolescents. At least 50 percent of the children served by these organizations must be living at or below the national poverty rate. An application must be submitted in order to receive books.

- **Half Price Books** is the largest family-owned retailer for new and used books, with more than 100 stores nationwide. Half Price Books accepts donation requests from certain 501(c)(3) nonprofit organizations and educators, but can only fulfill requests in areas where they currently operate.

As students have access to more books at home, it becomes important to help parents understand ways to use those books effectively with their children as well. Setting up literacy education events is a great way to share this information and give parents practice with these skills. Consider also providing resources such as the following:

- Phonics materials (e.g., magnetic letters and a magnetic board)
- Reading/literacy games
- Read aloud tips
- Journals for written response to reading
- Sight word cards/games

Food or Clothing Needs

According to the US Department of Agriculture, in 2022 approximately 17.3 percent of US households (6.4 million households, including 13 million children) were food insecure. In fact, families with children are more likely to face hunger, with Black and Latino families being twice as likely to experience hunger as other families. And although many students can qualify to receive breakfast and lunch at school, food availability for other meals is not guaranteed. Sometimes food pantry locations are the barrier if parents do not have reliable transportation or availability to get to the pantry. Partnering with a local food bank to house a pantry at your school can remove the barrier. Parents can visit the pantry when they pick up or drop off their children at school. High school students within the school or district can even be in charge of helping to organize and/or distribute the pantry items and receive community service hours needed for graduation requirements. Clothing and footwear needs can also be met in this way, by partnering with a local thrift store. This can be especially important during winter months.

Another way to help meet food needs is to provide parents who attend school activities with access to a free bag of groceries if they are in need of food. For example, the families who show up get bags of groceries. It's a great way to meet all parents where they are!

- **Feeding America** is the largest charity working to end hunger in the United States. It is part of a nationwide network of food banks, food pantries, and community-based organizations that focus on ending hunger. They also provide a vast set of resources to support feeding children and families including the ability to search their network for resources in your local area as well as how to start a food pantry in your school or district.

- **Feed the Children** is a leading hunger relief organization. In addition to providing food to children in nearly all fifty states, Feed the Children also provides essential items like shampoo, soap, toothpaste, and cleaning products. There are five distribution centers in the United States, which allows the organization to deliver resources to communities in both cities and rural areas to help families thrive. They also provide summer meal support and have an interactive map that families can use to find local food distribution centers during the summer months when the children are not in school.

Housing Needs

Housing instability, which includes difficulty paying rent, spending a significant amount of household income on housing, overcrowded living conditions, frequent moving, eviction, unsafe housing, or homelessness, can have a significant negative effect on youth and families' well-being in both the short- and long-term. Consider these facts: In 2023, nearly 583,000 people experienced homelessness across the United States, and 33 percent of those people were families with children or unaccompanied youth (aged twenty-five or younger) (National Alliance to End Homelessness, 2023). Currently, more than one-quarter of renter households spend more than half of their income on rent. These renters are disproportionately more likely to be individuals with disabilities and families with young children.

Stable housing is foundational for children and families in communities, enabling them to access opportunities that are necessary for them to succeed and build their futures. Research shows that stable housing leads to:

- Increased educational achievement and graduation rates and improved health outcomes

- Greater family stability, with stronger bonds between children and parents

- Increased capabilities for parents to participate in their children's school experience

- Improved access to jobs as well as resources and amenities, including public benefits programs

- Stronger communities as young people and families build greater ties to neighbors and the places they live (Annie E. Casey Foundation, 2020)

Funders for Housing and Opportunity (FHO) is a nationwide funder collaborative committed to improving stable housing options, especially for those who have historically been underserved or denied access. FHO has awarded nearly $23 million in grants across the country to support fair and equitable housing opportunities. Organizations can apply for grants by invitation or a formal RFP process.

Community Services Block Grant is a federally funded grant that provides funds to states, territories, and tribes to administer support services that alleviate the causes and conditions of poverty in under resourced communities. Grants are funded for services and activities including housing, nutrition, utility, and transportation assistance; and employment, education, and other income- and asset-building services.

National Center for Homeless Education has a helpful brief for homeless service providers and homeless education staff to help them understand their roles in supporting youth and families experiencing homelessness, while offering tools and strategies to enhance collaboration among agencies.

State Interagency Councils on Homelessness consist of cross-system member organizations to coordinate the homelessness strategy for their regions or states. They offer assistance to local leaders and providers, including educational agencies and boards of education.

LIVED AND LEARNED

You Get Farther When You Row the Boat in the Same Direction

▶ Housing partnerships for parents are typically available through the housing authority and your local city in many ways. We wanted to positively impact the homelessness rate in Topeka, so we decided to replicate what a neighboring community in Kansas City, Kansas, shared with us. They called their system Impact KCK and shared their outcomes of reducing homelessness by 50 percent (avenueoflife.org/impact-kck).

In order to have the greatest impact, the staff who created Impact KCK contacted Topeka and partnered to replicate their success. As a result, homelessness has declined in Topeka Public Schools. The organizers called the program Impact Avenues, and they knew the city would have to act as the backbone of the partnership. Through support from Impact KCK staff and the city of Topeka, they were able to coordinate funding from dozens of community organizations such as the United Way, local community-focused businesses, the

(Continued)

(Continued)

housing authority, and many other groups. Our district assigned our homeless coordinator to work with the program to help identified families ready to move out of homelessness through a specific screening process. Those families are then invited to an Impact Day, in which organizations that provide all of the needed social services and resources converge at one location on the same day. Examples include resources to support addiction recovery, domestic violence prevention, open employment opportunities, and affordable housing. This Impact Day helps to remove the wait time and access issues that are common barriers for individuals seeking to get out of homelessness. At the end of the Impact Day, each family leaves with keys to an affordable home and the initial resources they need for successful transition out of homelessness. Impact Avenues shows the power of what the collective capacity of involved community members can do. As a result of this partnership, Topeka Public Schools has decreased the homeless student population by more than 50 percent since 2016 (Impact Avenues, 2022). Additionally, 97 percent of families who have attained a permanent housing solution through Impact Avenues remain stably housed.

Financial Planning and Education Needs

According to research (Xiao, 2016), low-income consumers often lack familiarity with or exposure to financial resources, such as products, services, tools, and advice for financial planning and management. They also are more likely to be underserved by financial products and services that are safe, useful, affordable, and convenient. With typically fewer employment options, low-income adults are highly vulnerable to economic shifts and instability in housing or the labor market. This is especially true for non-English speakers and immigrants who do not yet understand the US financial system (National Endowment for Financial Education, 2016).

In partnership with local bank branches, credit unions, or other financial providers, schools can provide families with information and education to support their financial literacy and plan for the future. Important topics for education can include how to manage a budget, make good spending and saving decisions, grow wealth, receive credit counseling, file taxes and receive tax assistance, and plan for home ownership.

Financial literacy is especially important for families with children who have aspirations to attend college, including how to set up college savings accounts and apply for federal college aid. For example, according to the National Center for Educational Statistics (Bahr et al., 2018), only around 65 percent of high school seniors complete a FAFSA form each year. Local banks and financial institutions will work with schools and students to educate them on the importance of the application and how it can help make college affordable, and even help students and families complete the form.

However, true financial stability will not result in generational wealth without attention to financial education for children. EconEdLink (a service of the Council for Economic Education [CEE]) provides classroom financial literacy resources to educators in grades K–12. CEE also oversees a network of state councils and local centers in each state that provide teacher training, educational resources, and direct-to-student programming. By balancing programming, services, and support between families and students, we can better prepare our communities for financial success and independence.

Medical or Dental Services

Much like a food desert, a medical or dental desert is an area whose population does not have adequate access to medical/dental care. It is estimated that about 80 percent of counties across the United States lack adequate health care infrastructure in some form, which means that medical/dental deserts affect tens of millions of Americans (Chakraborty, 2022). Most medical/dental deserts are found in rural areas, but many urban areas are also affected when the infrastructure in place does not have enough providers to care for the community. This is especially true in low-income areas where many residents rely on Medicaid services, where the rate of coverage is left to the states and typically means low profit margin payouts for dentists and doctors (Childress, 2012).

As medical and dental services require specialization, finding a community partner to support this type of initiative is required. Mobile clinics are a way to connect vulnerable populations with access to health and dental care.

Mobile Health Map

Mobile Health Map is a database of mobile clinics in the United States (more than 3,000 nationwide). Members of this collaborative network supply information about their location, services, target populations, and costs. Their website can be used to find and schedule a mobile clinic at your school site.

School-based clinics are another way to provide health and dental services to students, and even the greater community. According to the 2022 National Census of School-Based Health conducted by the School-Based Health Alliance (SBHA), there are roughly 3,900 school-based health centers nationwide. The SBHA is a nonprofit that advocates for high-quality health care in schools for the nation's most vulnerable children. "Working at the intersection of healthcare and education, SBHA is a recognized leader in the school-based health care field and a source of information on best practices for philanthropic, federal, state, and local partners and policymakers" (School-Based Health Alliance, 2022). SBHA also provides services to support community and school partnerships that establish new school-based health centers or assess those already in existence.

 **LIVED AND LEARNED**

Site-Based Services Can Have a Significant Impact

▶ David Distler, principal of Eisenberg Elementary School in the Colonial School District in Delaware believed that students' untreated medical conditions and trauma was contributing to the school's poor attendance rates and discipline challenges. So when the district superintendent proposed opening a health clinic at Eisenberg, Distler was immediately on board.

The clinic launched in 2016, becoming Delaware's first health clinic in a traditional elementary school. It is housed in a converted classroom and contains one exam room, a counseling office, and a small lab that can run basic tests. Nemours Children's Health, a nonprofit that operates pediatric hospitals and clinics, staffs the clinic at Eisenberg with nurse practitioners, social workers, and a psychologist.

Parents can bring children to the clinic during operating hours, but school staff can also refer students for health services or ask a clinician to intervene in instances where unmet health needs arise, such as if a student's unmanaged illness causes frequent absences. Since the opening of the clinic, attendance rates have improved and the number of "discipline referrals" for serious misbehavior decreased dramatically from 1,000 annually when Distler first arrived at Eisenberg to approximately 100 per year now.

Attendance

Although missing one or two days of school here and there may not really seem to matter, as anyone who has spent time around school children knows, consistency is key. When children consistently miss school, they are not only missing out on vital learning opportunities, but also on opportunities to be part of the school community, to build lasting friendships, and to build social skills necessary to succeed outside the classroom. Physical presence in school as well as feelings of connectedness at school are also major supports for students struggling with mental health. "Youth who felt connected to adults and peers at school were significantly less likely than those who did not to report persistent feelings of sadness or hopelessness (35% vs. 53%); that they seriously considered attempting suicide (14% vs. 26%); or attempted suicide (6% vs. 12%)" (Centers for Disease Control and Prevention, 2022). Consider the attendance statistics listed in Figure 4.1.

For most children, getting to school on time, or attending school at all, is out of their control. As a school leader, it is important to understand this yourself as well as make sure that teachers understand this, so as not to blame the children. Ultimately, in order to change student attendance habits, we

FIGURE 4.1 Impact of Student Absences

CHILD MISSING JUST . . .	THAT EQUALS . . .	WHICH IS . . .	OVER 13 YEARS OF SCHOOLING THAT'S . . .
30 minutes per day	Nearly half a day per week	4 weeks per year	1 year of school
1 hour per day	Nearly 1 day per week	8 weeks per year	2 years of school
2 days per month	20 days per year	4 weeks per year	1 year of school
4 days per month	40 days per year	8 weeks per year	2 years of school

have to figure out what the underlying causes are for the absences and seek to remove those barriers or provide assistance. Frequent phone calls and/or porch visits (where a member of the school staff visits the home) are a good way to begin this communication. Once the root cause(s) is identified, then creative problem solving can begin in order to alleviate the barrier. If you do not have the capacity within your school or district to accommodate this kind of correspondence and family support, the support of a community organization or partnership may be necessary.

LIVED AND LEARNED

There's A Story Behind Student Absences

▶ The research is clear: Being in school is important. Children who are chronically absent in the early grades are much less likely to read at grade level by third grade, making them four times more likely to drop out of high school. Students can only benefit from the many resources school offers and can succeed academically if they are present.

Attendance at Belshire Elementary School in Tennessee was low, especially since the COVID-19 pandemic. The principal recognized that outside assistance was needed in order to turn this challenge around. Parents needed to be educated about the importance of school attendance, accountability for attendance needed to be put in place, and struggling families needed assistance when attendance barriers were identified. So, Belshire decided to partner with Communities in Schools (CIS), a national organization that utilizes a school-based approach to developing academic success by tackling academic and nonacademic barriers. Site coordinators assess a student's needs and then provide direct services

(Continued)

(Continued)

and/or make referrals to community partners to ensure a student has everything they need to succeed in and out of the classroom. At Belshire, the CIS site coordinator has a specific caseload of students with chronic absenteeism to help them (and their families) get the services needed for the students to be present and prepared in school. Since implementing the CIS partnership, chronic absenteeism dropped from 41 percent to 36 percent over the course of the 2021–2022 school year (Communities in Schools, 2023).

What I have also learned over time from far too many personal experiences is to pay attention to the story behind the absenteeism data. There is a difference between a student who is absent often and a student who is absent multiple days in a row. The story behind a student who is absent or tardy at various times but without any consistent type of pattern may be about transportation challenges or parents whose work schedules do not allow for them to hold the student accountable for showing up at the bus stop on time every day. But the story behind a child who is absent two or more days in a row without a parent contacting the school is usually much deeper. It often means there's been some sort of change or challenge in the family—financial work-related challenges, domestic issues, sudden illness, parent incarceration, home eviction, death in the family, and so forth. This is why in places where I have served, we have implemented an attendance protocol focused on relationships. While the district policy for truancy may allow multiple days out of school before the school initiates home contact, the practices carried out by the school leader can convey a deeper sense of urgency. If a child is absent two or more days in a row without a parent contacting the school, it warrants a home visit. This means that social workers, counselors, and educators visit and call homes on a regular basis as part of our larger system to address chronic absenteeism while also addressing the social determinants of health within the community. Our approach had reduced chronic absenteeism in Topeka by 20 percent before the pandemic.

If the reason behind the child's absence is not a result of a significant barrier, it gives us the opportunity to talk with the parent and build their understanding of the importance of their child's presence in school. If we learn there is a significant barrier (whether new, unexpected, or chronic), it allows us to invest in our families as an extended school family and assist with addressing those deeper issues. It also helps us better know how to care for the child when they return to school, especially if we need to provide some additional services—counseling, mental health support, extra time to make up work, etc.

DMV Services

For many homeless and vulnerable populations of people, especially working poor with multiple jobs or those with unreliable access to transportation or the internet, utilizing Department of Motor Vehicles (DMV) services can be extremely challenging, if not impossible. Julie Janis, a social services director in New Jersey, works with homeless people and advocates regularly for access to state-issued identification cards. Janis says, "You cannot get housing without it. You cannot get any social services, general assistance, food stamps, social security, employment, a bank account, can't go to the doctor, rehab" (Burga, 2021). The list goes on and on. To combat this, our staff partnered with the DMV. The DMV set up mobile services that will come to any location throughout cities and towns, including schools, and essentially bring the DMV to those who need it most. By hosting a mobile DMV at a school location, you open the door to both families and students to obtain necessary services. This can be especially impactful for high school students who may need identification to get a job or apply for a driver's license but otherwise don't have the means to do so.

PUBLICIZING PARTNERSHIPS AND RESOURCES

It doesn't matter how great the partnership is or how many identified needs it meets if no one knows that it exists. In order for families to utilize the available resources, services, or partnerships you put in place, you need to share information about it in places your families will look. For example, if your families do not often read the newspaper, have access to the internet, or read materials that come home, consider sharing information through other venues, such as at an info table during sporting matches or on a digital school marquee in front of the building. You can also share information with families through newsletters, text messages, or automated phone calls.

Figure 4.2 shows a sample of a weekly digital newsletter distributed to parents via email and text. Principal Gabrielle Tanner has tripled her parent involvement by sharing needed resources and engaging parents in her school as she provides these resources. Not only does her newsletter include information about upcoming school events, healthy sleep and attendance information, and school lunch menus, but it also contains a wealth of community resources, including car seat safety, an application for need-based assistance with the holidays, and a link to food pantry locations.

> ### Sustainable Partnerships: Programs vs. Systems
>
> Partnerships cannot start and end with the people who had the vision. There must be a shared collective vision that creates a system with an inter-reliance on many resources coming together so the system does not collapse with the removal of one leader or even the budget. Programs come and go with the leader, the budget, and that leader's vision. Systems will outlast the initial founders who helped create them because the vision is shared, the resources are dependent on partners co-creating new opportunities, and they are not dependent on one person or one organization. If you want to create for sustainability, bring the imagination and creativity of others together and they can produce a masterpiece with many interconnected elements that lasts a lifetime.

FIGURE 4.2 Sample Weekly Newsletter

SHELDON UPDATE

SHELDON'S WEEKLY FAMILY NEWSLETTER – 10.23.23

WELCOME FROM MRS. TANNER

Dear Sheldon Families,

We are excited to see all of you at Parent/Teacher Conferences this Wednesday & Thursday! Remember, there is NO SCHOOL this Thursday and Friday.

Click here to access the 2023-2024 Family Handbook.

As always, if you have questions or concerns, do not hesitate to reach out to me!

Thank you for the privilege of serving you ~
Mrs. Gabrielle Tanner, Principal

UPCOMING EVENTS

OCTOBER EVENTS

October is Audiology Awareness Month, Celebrating the Bilingual Child Month, and Principal Appreciation Month

October 24: Pumpkin Patch Field Trip
October 25: Parent/Teacher Conferences @ 4:00-8:00
October 26: NO SCHOOL - Parent/Teacher Conferences @ 8:00-8:00
October 27: NO SCHOOL
October 31: Fall Festival & Costume Parade - details below

Community Resources

Christmas Bureau

Click here for more information and to apply for the Christmas Bureau.

To Apply for Help
- You must live in Shawnee County. No exceptions.
- At least one adult from your household must apply in person on one of the four intake dates. There is no online intake.
- Everyone living at the same address must register on the same application.
- One adult can register the entire household.
- Registering adult MUST BRING:

-his/her Photo ID

-Proof of Income for the ENTIRE household

-everyone's Social Security cards (copies or document with SSN number listed are okay)

Christmas Bureau Intake Dates
There is only one location this year:

Echo Ridge Community Center 2021 SE Market St.

Use Topeka Metro Route 4

Wednesday, October 25

10:00 am – 7:00 pm

Monday, October 30

10:00 am – 7:00 pm

Thursday, November 2

10:00 am – 7:00 pm

Saturday, November 4 LAST DAY

10:00 am – 2:00 pm

Documentation for Proof of Income
Any State assistance or money received for food, rent, etc. is considered income. Bring copies that apply to your household. VISION cards are not proof, you MUST show the award letter from the State.

APPLICATIONS WILL NOT BE PROCESSED WITHOUT ALL REQUIRED DOCUMENTATION. See the flyer for complete information.

Topeka Resources Checklist

Take a look at the Topeka Resources Checklist. This is very helpful for planning! This is a list of possible resources to help you stretch your dollars and avoid economic emergencies.

(Continued)

(Continued)

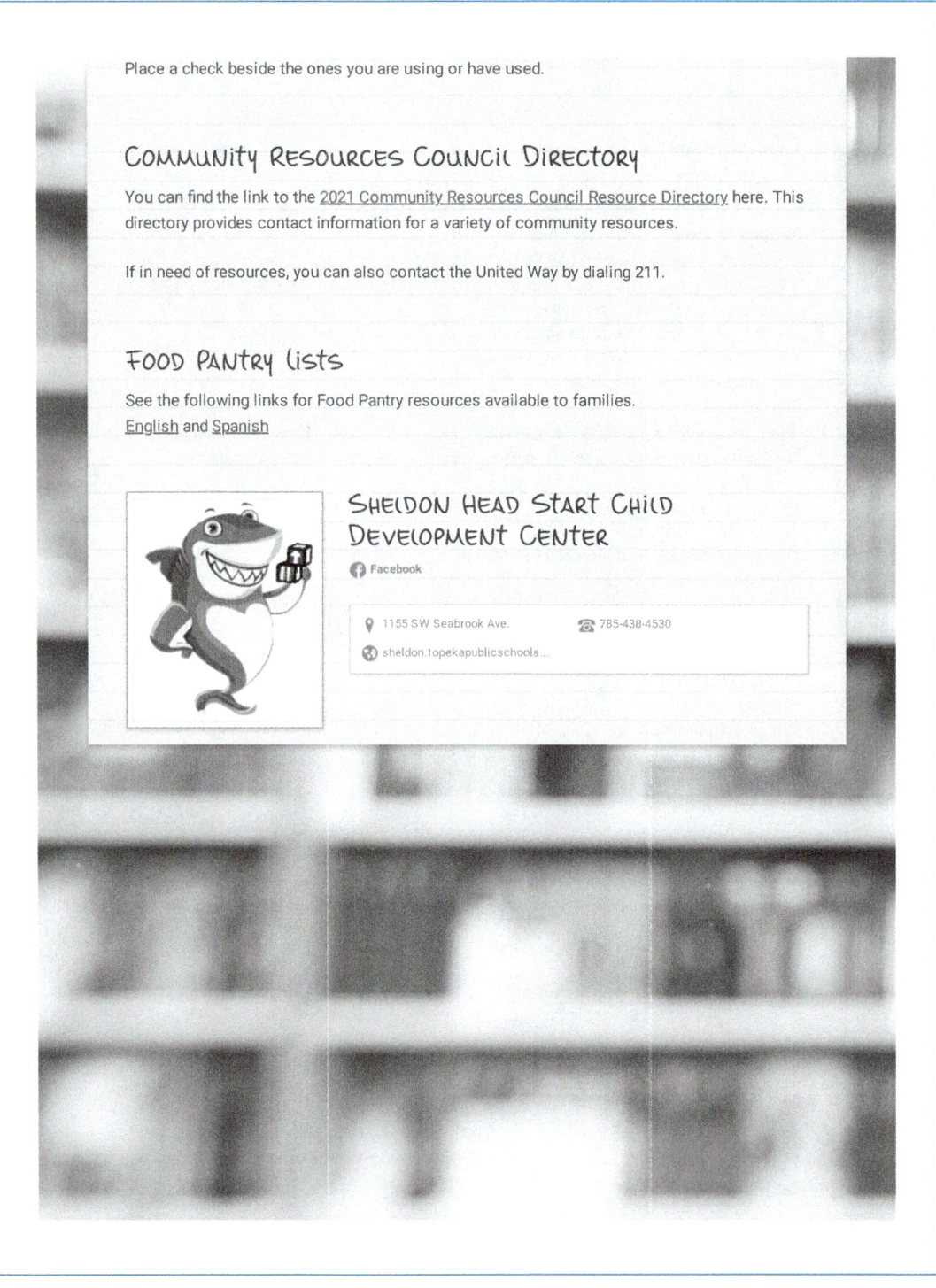

Place a check beside the ones you are using or have used.

COMMUNITY RESOURCES COUNCIL DIRECTORY

You can find the link to the 2021 Community Resources Council Resource Directory here. This directory provides contact information for a variety of community resources.

If in need of resources, you can also contact the United Way by dialing 211.

FOOD PANTRY Lists

See the following links for Food Pantry resources available to families.
English and Spanish

SHELDON HEAD START CHILD DEVELOPMENT CENTER

Facebook

1155 SW Seabrook Ave.   785-438-4530

sheldon.topekapublicschools...

SOURCE: Gabrielle Tanner

In addition to using traditional methods of communication, consider other nontraditional venues, such as at popular local restaurants, churches, or in your community grocery stores. Local radio stations and movie theaters typically also offer free or discounted ad space that can be used to share information about available resources, partnerships, upcoming events, general good news or great things related to your school or students/families, or other important information. By utilizing locations within your community, you are opening the door for people outside of your direct school "family" to learn more and see the school as the center of the community. You are also creating awareness about school-community partnerships, which is indirect advocacy and marketing for those businesses as well.

> Parents tend to trust the voice and opinion of other parents. Consider creating a team of parents to make short videos about resources or programs available at your school. These videos can then be shared or distributed strategically through platforms such as social media, during parent meetings on campus, on the school's YouTube channel, and more!

Promoting Positive Parenting

Although building parent capacity and focusing on the school as the center of the community are the main reasons for publicizing information, you can also use it as a way to dispel stereotypes and break down walls and misperceptions among other populations within your community about the diverse families you serve.

Educating the community about the parents being served is particularly important when the socioeconomic levels across the community vary greatly or when a segment of the demographics within the community are senior citizens who have not been in schools for decades. Providing demographic data and sharing the success stories with the community can help diminish stereotypes that may otherwise be created based on what individuals may hear or learn from their primary media source for information. For example, often there are stereotypes regarding low-income parents being unemployed, when in actuality, many parents in poverty are the working poor. According to the US Bureau of Labor and Statistics (2023), "In 2021, 3.3 million families were living below the poverty level despite having at least one member in the labor force for half the year or more." Social media or other creative outlets can be used to highlight the diverse parent population you serve and share the stories of parents who are business owners, to share success stories of parents who are engaged in schools and the community, to display photos of parents being engaged with their children or reading to their children, and to demonstrate how parents are partnering with the school. Such messages also set the expectations of what parent engagement looks like in your school and can break down stereotypes. Even more compelling are short, parent-created testimonial videos about ways they are engaged in the school, have used school resources, or have benefited from school-community partnerships.

Give Them Something Positive to Talk About

▶ It is no secret that news media outlets tend to cover stories they think will attract the largest viewership. It's not that they don't want to cover nice stories or great things happening in schools, but poor test scores, child tragedy, or controversial policies often dominate the messages shared and get more attention when it comes to media coverage in schools. However, schools can be a resource that gives a new message, dominating what media receives from your school or district. One way the districts I have served changed the negative narrative was to intentionally share information in a systematic way. So, every week we send a top ten list highlighting at least ten positive staff, parent, and student partnership stories to local, state, and national news outlets and media partners. The list typically includes official press releases or news articles we write for the school district website, speakers or events happening at schools throughout the district, or exciting things parents or students are doing to support the community. Not everything gets picked up or reported on, but our hope is that if we can make it easy for the news to report on the good things, we will positively impact our community and make sure they don't only hold a negative mindset about what our schools and families are all about.

Figure 4.3 shows a snapshot from a recent "good news" release.

FIGURE 4.3 Good News Release

Upcoming Stories for the Week		
October 30, 2023		
TPS Media Contact:		
Dr. Aarion L. Gray		
agray@tps501.org		
POSSIBLE NEWS STORY	**DATE/TIME/PLACE**	**CONTACT**
Topeka Public Schools Students Enjoy Fall Parades & Parties	On Tuesday, October 31, TPS Superintendent Dr. Tiffany Anderson will drop by several schools for fall parades and parties, as schools across the district hold celebrations. • McCarter Elementary Parade at 9:15 AM (5512 SW 16th St) • Meadows Elementary Parade at 2:00 PM (201 SW Clay) • Shaner Early Learning Academy Parade at 2:15 PM (1600 SW 34th St)	Dr. Aarion L. Gray

POSSIBLE NEWS STORY	DATE/TIME/PLACE	CONTACT
Topeka West High School Hosts Local Candidate Forum	**Date:** Friday, November 3, 2023 **Time:** 9:23 AM–10:06 AM **Location:** Topeka West High School (2001 SW Fairlawn Rd) Auditorium On November 3, Topeka West High School will host a local candidate forum for students, staff, families, and members of the community. The event will feature all candidates running for USD 501 Board of Education, as well as District 8 City Council.	Dr. Aarion L. Gray
"Granny Nancy" Returns to Quincy as a Volunteer After Graduating From the School Decades Ago	Nancy High, better known as Granny Nancy, is a volunteer at Quincy Elementary School. The Quincy children ABSOLUTELY love her. She spends her time with us, wiping down lunch tables, talking with students, and usually has her arms wide open because a child is running to give her a hug. During lunchtime it never fails that you will hear a student say, "Hey Granny . . . . Look at this! Granny . . . . did you know . . . . ?" But what makes Granny Nancy truly special is she is a Quincy graduate herself! In fact, at 82 years young she has brought in her school pictures to share with the students. Quincy staff say they are so thankful that such a dear woman chooses to spend a few hours with them each week and chooses to give back to the school that was once part of her childhood education. Wiping down lunch tables might seem like a trivial job, but it is so much more. It brings a bright smile, a warm heart, and a bunch of vintage Quincy love through the door every week.	Dr. Aarion L. Gray
Topeka Public Schools Parents as Teachers Earns Endorsement as Blue Ribbon Affiliate	On October 23, Topeka Public Schools Parents as Teachers Program earned another endorsement as a Blue Ribbon Affiliate! Parents as Teachers is a free, evidence-based program that connects parents with children ages 0-5 with resources to raise a child that is healthy, safe, and ready for school. TPS Parents as Teachers provides Group Connections meetings, personal visits, and access to the Community Cupboard to help with clothing, hygiene items, food, and more.	Dr. Aarion L. Gray

(Continued)

POSSIBLE NEWS STORY	DATE/TIME/PLACE	CONTACT
	This award affirms we are one of the top performing home visiting affiliates in the PAT National Center's international network.

To help ensure that Parents as Teachers affiliates are achieving fidelity to the Parents as Teachers model and facilitate continuous quality improvements—and children and families are thereby receiving the highest quality services possible—Parents as Teachers developed the Quality Endorsement and Improvement Process. Parents as Teachers affiliates are required to engage in the Quality Endorsement and Improvement Process in their fourth year of implementation and every five years thereafter.

To earn the Quality Endorsement, affiliates must complete a comprehensive self-study and review process that demonstrates they are meeting or exceeding the Parents as Teachers Essential Requirements, along with at least 80 percent of the Quality Standards.

Programs that earn the Quality Endorsement are recognized by the national Parents as Teachers office as exemplary Blue Ribbon Affiliates, delivering high-quality services to children and families.

Congratulations! parents as teachers
BLUE RIBBON AFFILIATE

Through the successful completion of the Quality Endorsement and Improvement Process,

Topeka Public Schools – USD#501

is hereby recognized as a Blue Ribbon Affiliate.

October 1, 2023 – September 30, 2028

Constance Gully
President and Chief Executive Officer
Parents as Teachers National Center

Allison L. Kemner
Senior Vice President and Chief Research Officer
Parents as Teachers National Center | |
| **Topeka High School Hosts USD 501 Board of Education Candidate Meet & Greet** | **Date:** Wednesday, November 1, 2023
Time: 5:30–7:00 PM
Location: Topeka High School (800 SW 10th Ave)

On November 1, Topeka High School will host a Meet & Greet for students, families, and community members to learn more about all of the candidates running for USD 501 Board of Education. | Dr. Aarion L. Gray |

POSSIBLE NEWS STORY	DATE/TIME/PLACE	CONTACT
Topeka Public Schools Celebrates Native American Heritage Month & Hosts Indigenous Family Night	**Date:** Month of November **Various Times & Locations** Topeka Public Schools is celebrating Native American Heritage all month long. We want to take this time to recognize our Native American students, staff, and families. We will be sharing how our families celebrate their culture as well as their traditions. On **Thursday, November 2, 2023 at 5:30 PM** the Topeka Public Schools Board of Education will recognize this important celebration with the reading of a proclamation. A presentation will be given by Mr. Yale Taylor, who serves as the district's Consulting Teacher for Native American Studies. **On November 13, 2023 from 5:30 - 6:30 PM, Topeka Public Schools will host its annual fall Indigenous Family Night at Jardine Middle School.** Artist Lisa Baker will guide student and families in creating Cherokee Corn Husk Dolls. Additional events and learning will take place at individual schools. *public schools* **Indigenous FAMILY NIGHT** **November 13, 2023** **5:30 - 6:30 PM** **Jardine Middle School** Artist Lisa Baker will guide students & families in creating Cherokee Corn Husk Dolls. Pizza will be provided!	Dr. Aarion L. Gray

(Continued)

CHAPTER 4 • BUILDING CAPACITY THROUGH POWERFUL PARTNERSHIPS 87

(Continued)

POSSIBLE NEWS STORY	DATE/TIME/PLACE	CONTACT
Scots Theater to open 2023-24 Season With "Fall One Act Festival"	**View Press Release** Scots Theater at Highland Park High School is proud and excited to return to the stage with their first-ever Fall One Act Festival, November 10th and 11th, 2023. The performances will start at 7:00 PM in the auditorium of Highland Park High School, 2424 SE California Ave. Donations will be accepted at both performances. The Fall One Act Festival is a collection of short one-act performances directed by new Scots Theater director, Kara McCormick, assisted by Cory Deeds-Rookstool. A troupe of 12 actors, assisted by a talented backstage team, will work together in different combinations to perform six shows that range from the comical and absurd to dramatic and serious. "The opportunity for our students to get back on stage is simply marvelous and I hope that our community will join us as Scots Theater begins a new era," says Deeds-Rookstool. "The cast and crew have enjoyed working on such an interesting collection of tales as well." "The shows give us an opportunity to show our talents in new and original ways", says David Jimenez, a junior at HPHS. For more information, to set up further contact with the cast and crew, or for photos, please contact Scots Theater at kmccormick@tps501.org.	Dr. Aarion L. Gray
Topeka West High School Hosts Local Candidate Forum	**Date:** Friday, November 3, 2023 **Time:** 9:23 AM–10:06 AM **Location:** Topeka West High School (2001 SW Fairlawn Rd) Auditorium On November 3, Topeka West High School will host a local candidate forum for students, staff, families, and members of the community. The event will feature all candidates running for USD 501 Board of Education, as well as District 8 City Council.	Dr. Aarion L. Gray
Topeka West Theatre Department Hosts Community Fall Fun Day	**Date:** Sunday, November 5, 2023 **Time:** 2:00–5:00 PM **Location:** Topeka West High School (2001 SW Fairlawn Rd)	

BUILDING PARENT CAPACITY IN HIGH-POVERTY SCHOOLS

POSSIBLE NEWS STORY	DATE/TIME/PLACE	CONTACT
	On November 5, the Topeka West High School Theatre Department will host a Fall Fun Day to support their activities this school year. The event is open to all in the community and is ideal for children aged 5–10. It will include games, face painting, and arts and crafts, and the cost is $10 per child. Topeka West Theatre **FALL FUN DAY** 11/5/2023. 2:00 P.M.– 5:00 P.M. TOPEKA WEST HIGH SCHOOL CAMPUS QUAD GAMES, FACE PAINTING, ARTS AND CRAFTS. IDEAL FOR AGES 5-10 $10 PER CHILD Parents must accompany their child All Proceeds Benefit the Theatre Department	Dr. Aarion L. Gray
TPS College Prep Academy Hosts Guest Speakers for Native American Heritage Month Celebration	**Date:** Wednesday, November 8, 2023 **Time:** 9:00 AM **Location:** TCALC (500 SW Tuffy Kellogg Dr) On November 8, Topeka Public Schools College Prep Academy will host three guest speakers to share their experiences as indigenous people, in celebration of Native American Heritage Month. There will be a three-station rotation with the three guest speakers, with each lasting 15 minutes to allow for intimate conversation and questions. Everyone will come together for 5 minutes at the end of the event. Our guest speakers will be Christina Haswood, Kansas State Legislator for District 10 and member of the Navajo Nations, Dr. Dee Ann Deroin of the University of Missouri-Kansas City, a Med School Recruiter, and our very own Mr. Yale Taylor, the Consulting Teacher for Native American Education for Topeka Public Schools.	Dr. Aarion L. Gray

(Continued)

(Continued)

POSSIBLE NEWS STORY	DATE/TIME/PLACE	CONTACT
Topeka High School Holds Annual Marine Corps Ball	**Date:** Saturday, November 11, 2023 **Time:** 6:00 PM **Location:** Topeka High School (800 SW 10th St) Topeka High School JROTC is hosting its annual Marine Corps Ball for cadets on Saturday, November 11. The event celebrates the birthday of the Marine Corps, which was founded over 248 years ago. It is also a way to remember and thank all of the members of the Marine Corps who have served.	Dr. Aarion Gray
Topeka High Trojan Theatre Presents Nevermore! The Imaginary Life & Mysterious Death of Edgar Allan Poe	**Date:** November 16–18, 2023 **Time:** 7:00 PM **Location:** Topeka High School (800 SW 10th Ave) Topeka High School presents the fall Trojan Theatre production Nevermore! The Imaginary Life & Mysterious Death of Edgar Allan Poe. Show dates are November 16-18 at 7:00 PM in the THS Auditorium. Tickets are $10 for general admission and $8 for students with ID. 	Dr. Aarion L. Gray

POSSIBLE NEWS STORY	DATE/TIME/PLACE	CONTACT
Topeka Public Schools Celebrates School Psychology Week	**Date:** November 6–10, 2023 **Various times & locations** During the week of November 6–10, Topeka Public Schools is recognizing our amazing school psychologists! Topeka Public Schools makes mental health a priority, and school psychologists work daily to ensure the district provides students and staff with the support they need to thrive in and out of school. Our school psychologists and their teams provide referrals, resources, counseling, classroom instruction, and much more. Additionally, the Topeka Public Schools Board of Education will honor school psychologists across the district at their meeting on **Thursday, November 16**.	Dr. Aarion L. Gray
TPS Hosts Educators for Night Out at Bishop, Featuring Key Note Speaker Dr. Alex Red Corn	**Date:** Thursday, November 9, 2023 **Time:** 3:30–6:30 PM **Location:** Bishop Professional Development Center (3601 SW 31st St) Topeka Public Schools staff are invited to attend the Night Out at Bishop, a professional learning event at Bishop Professional Development Center (3601 SW 31st St) on Thursday, November 9 from 3:30-6:30 PM. The Night Out at Bishop will feature keynote speaker Dr. Alex Red Corn from the Kansas State University Department of Educational Leadership and exciting breakout sessions covering a variety of topics in the areas of technology, curriculum, and instruction. • Using Artificial Intelligence in the Classroom • Hands-On Learning • Enhancing Engagement & Creating Student Ownership • Culturally Responsive Celebrations • iPads & Native Language • Incorporating Diverse Books Into Instruction • Digging Into Clarity, Discussions, & Questioning • Building Thinking Classrooms for All Content Areas Prize drawings will also take place throughout the event!	Dr. Aarion L. Gray

(Continued)

(Continued)

POSSIBLE NEWS STORY	DATE/TIME/PLACE	CONTACT
Topeka Public Schools Students & Staff Honor Those Who Have Served on Veterans Day	**Date:** Friday, November 10, 2023 **Various Times & Locations** Topeka Public Schools students and staff across the district will be honoring military veterans and thanking them for their service throughout the day on Veterans Day. Demonstrations will take place at Topeka West High School, Topeka High School, and Highland Park High School, courtesy of JROTC, which represents all branches of the US military. McEachron Elementary School also hosts an annual all-school assembly featuring music and a student performance from the Growth Mindset Unicycle Club.	Dr. Aarion Gray

POSSIBLE NEWS STORY	DATE/TIME/PLACE	CONTACT
Topeka Public Schools Celebrates American Education Week	**Date:** November 14–18, 2023 **Various Times & Locations** American Education Week, which will be celebrated November 14–18, 2023, will present all Americans with a wonderful opportunity to celebrate public education and honor individuals who are making a difference in ensuring that every child receives a quality education. Topeka Public Schools works all year round to make sure our students get the best education possible. During the pandemic, education evolved and looks a little different, so we want to show special appreciation for our educators and their resilience, creativity, and optimism. During American Education Week, we will be giving special shout-outs to educators who are making a difference in students' lives. **Activities include:** • 11/13: Kickoff Day • 11/14: Family Day • 11/15: Education Support Professionals Day • 11/16: Principal for a Day • 11/17: Substitute Educators Day	Dr. Aarion L. Gray
Legislators & Community Leaders Learn What It's Like to be "Principal for a Day" at Topeka Public Schools	**Date:** Thursday, November 16, 2023 **Time/Location:** 10:00–12:00 PM at schools across the district - *additional information coming soon!* Topeka Public Schools is excited to host legislators, community leaders, and industry professionals from across Shawnee County for the annual Principal for a Day event. This annual event allows each individual to shadow a principal at one of the district's schools for one hour and then attend a virtual luncheon to debrief and learn more about Topeka Public Schools. Principal for a Day will host members of the Kansas State Legislature, as well as representatives from the City of Topeka Government, Kansas State Department of Education, and many others!	Dr. Aarion L. Gray

(Continued)

(Continued)

POSSIBLE NEWS STORY	DATE/TIME/PLACE	CONTACT
Topeka Public Schools Hosts College Fine Arts Fair at TCALC	**Date:** Friday, November 17, 2023 **Time:** 9:30 - 11:00 AM & 12:00–1:30 PM **Location:** TCALC (500 SW Tuffy Kellogg Dr) On November 17, Topeka Public Schools will host its annual College Fine Arts Fair at the Topeka Center for Advanced Learning & Careers (TCALC). Students will have the opportunity to learn about pursuing, continuing, or participating in fine arts during college. Faculty members and admissions counselors will be available for auditions, portfolio review, and to answer any questions students may have. Students do not need to be a fine arts major to take advantage of fine arts classes and scholarships! **Participating colleges and universities include:** • Baker University • Butler Community College • Emporia State University • Fort Hays State University • Friends University • MidAmerica Nazarene University • Ottawa University • Pittsburg State University • University of Kansas • Washburn University • Wichita State University	Dr. Aarion L. Gray

SOURCE: Aarion L. Gray

POWERFUL PARTNERSHIPS IN ACTION

Oakland Unified School District has one of the most diverse racial, ethnic, and linguistic student populations of anywhere in the United States. Serving approximately 35,000 students, about 75 percent of them are eligible for free or reduced price lunch. In order to best serve Oakland's diverse population, in 2010 the school district committed to following a full-service community schools approach to build parent and community capacity and positively impact student outcomes. As a result, the district completely reorganized itself to prioritize the initiative and established a Community Schools and Student Services department. The strategic plan for the initiative outlines the mission as follows:

"For us to reach our vision, our mission must be to forcibly eliminate inequities by ensuring those who we have historically most marginalized are provided expanded and enhanced real-world learning opportunities, addressing barriers to learning by creating safe, healthy and welcoming operationalizing equity, not just talking about it. Schools need to partner with families and communities to create the education our students deserve. . . . Community schools are about operationalizing equity, not just talking about it" (Klevan et al., 2023, p. 11).

As this initiative has taken hold, schools across the district have increased resources available to help them create lasting community partnerships that support families and students. For example, currently sixty schools across the district now have linkages to school-based health centers, which provide medical, dental, vision, and behavioral health services to students and families. The initiative has also increased schools' ability to partner with high-quality organizations to offer after-school programming for academics, enrichment, and adult education. There is also an emphasis on restorative justice practices to build more positive school climates.

As a result of the initiative and community partnerships, parent engagement and feelings of welcome and value have increased. Student graduation rates also improved from 59 percent in 2011 to 73 percent in 2019.

POWERFUL PARTNERSHIPS REFLECTION

Think back to what you read throughout this chapter. Use these reflection questions to consider your own school or district and the role you play in building parent capacity.

1. How does your school or district typically address barriers for parental engagement?

2. What types of partnerships exist at your school or district?

3. Are there partnerships with businesses or community organizations in your local area that could be occurring but are not?

4. What type of approach could you use to gain more support from businesses or community organizations in your local area?

Take some time to reflect on your learning and plan for action in your next steps.

WHAT?

Summarize your learning and key takeaways from this chapter.

SO WHAT?

Record ideas about how your key takeaways apply to you, your school, and/or your district.

NOW WHAT?

Based on your key takeaways, plan your next steps for moving forward in this area.

CHAPTER 5

Funding the Promise of a Better Future

"If you think education is expensive, try ignorance."

—Landers (1975)

Strategic school funding is critical because it changes the vision of how needs are met. "A fair, equitable, and adequate school funding formula is the basic building block of a well-resourced and academically successful school system for all students" (Education Law Center, 2020). Throughout my career, I have visited hundreds of schools across the country. I have met great teachers and educational leaders in schools and districts who found themselves frustrated over the challenges that stem from lack of funding or lack of vision in how to strategically use funding to support the needs in their schools. Every system and organization that serves people needs resources to successfully do so. School systems are in the business of educating children and, thus, improving the lives of families. Like any business, staff must be hired and resources must be provided in order to serve well the students, and ultimately, families whose lives depend on it. In order to serve anyone well, it is critical to strategically use what you have in order to impact what you need to do.

The importance of school funding goes beyond just academic success. McKillip and Luhm (2020) note, "Explaining why resources need to be directed to schools serving low-income students requires an understanding of the profound impact poverty has on students' lives and their access to opportunities to learn. Along with a lack of financial resources, low-income parents and guardians are less likely to be able to access programs and activities to improve their children's academic skills. They are also more likely to be impacted by low-wage jobs with long and/or odd hours, lack of job security, and limited access to benefits such as paid time off and adequate health care." One study reported that "event-study and instrumental variable models reveal that a 10 percent increase in per-pupil spending each year for all twelve years of public school leads to 0.27 more completed years of education, 7.25 percent higher wages, and a 3.67 percentage-point reduction in the annual incidence of adult poverty; effects are much more pronounced for children from low-income families. Exogenous spending increases were associated with sizable improvements in measured school quality, including reductions in student-to-teacher ratios, increases in teacher salaries, and longer school years" (Jackson et al., 2015).

If a state spends $1,220 per year more to educate a low-income student (a 10 percent increase in the national average of $12,201 in 2017), then over twelve years that student represents an additional cost of $14,640.

That student is estimated to go on to earn a 9.6 percent higher salary. Based on the median national salary of $31,562 in 2017, over an average career of thirty years, that is $3,030 per year more, or an additional benefit of $90,900 (McKillip & Luhm, 2020).

Before we dive any further into the funding conversation, reflect on the schools you have visited or worked in. Think about how those schools operate and what student outcomes are achieved/produced. What factors account for potential differences in student outcome? What are the barriers? Often the *vision* for how to use resources is what makes the difference in the systems/programs that are funded or how barriers to school improvement are removed.

CREATING CHANGE THROUGH THE BUDGET

Understanding how schools are funded and how to creatively think outside the box when it comes to budgets and spending is important for school leaders as well as parents and can drastically help change what's done in schools to build parent capacity and improve outcomes for students. We can use the acronym *BUDGET* in thinking of key action steps to take.

Build personal understanding of school funding and finance

Use funds efficiently and find creative sources

Differentiate between high-priority needs and focus on solutions

Garner support by sharing stories well

Empower and educate families on school funding

Train and retain high-quality educators

B: Build Personal Understanding of School Funding

In more than twenty-five years of school leadership, I have never met a leader who stated they have more than enough funding for schools to change outcomes. I will be the first to tell you that funding alone will not change outcomes even when great leadership exists. Nonetheless, how funding is used and gained does impact what's available for students, their parents, and ultimately the community, so having a good understanding of how schools are funded, what funds can be spent on, and where to get additional funds is important.

In his book *Does Money Matter?*, Burtless (1996) of the Brookings Institution outlined the large spending inequities across states and within states that directly impact student achievement. His research focused on outcomes in the 1990s, which continue today with even greater disparity. Burtless found, "about 46% of public spending on elementary and secondary schools is derived from local and government budgets." The economic gap between communities has increased, resulting in even greater gaps in academic outcomes. Simply put, the wealthier the community, the higher the housing values, and the more businesses in a community that pay taxes, the more funding is generated to benefit public schools within the community. Conversely, the lower the income generated from businesses and housing values, the lower the tax base and funding rates for public schools in those communities.

School funding is also distributed in part based on student enrollment. Based on this model, the smaller the district, the fewer the resources available. Likewise, a system with lower per pupil revenue/expenditures, will have fewer resources available in the classroom, changing the quality of educators and resources students have access to in the classroom.

Allegretto, Garcia, and Weiss echo these findings in their 2022 Economic Policy Institute publication. They share, "Districts in high-poverty areas, which serve larger shares of students of color, get less funding per student than districts in low-poverty areas, which predominantly serve White students, highlighting the system's inequity. School districts in general—but especially those in high-poverty areas—are not spending enough to achieve national average test scores, which is an established benchmark for assessing adequacy. Efforts states make to invest in education vary significantly." For example, "[m]ajority Black districts receive, on average, a greater portion of their funding from state sources (31% vs. 14%)," which are susceptible to funding changes depending on elected officials and political policies, "while majority White districts draw more from local sources (82% vs. 58%)" (Allegretto et al., 2022).

These data hold true in Missouri, where my career in education began. Some districts spend about $7,000 per student while other districts spend more than $11,000. In the publication, *Still Separate, Still Unequal*, the authors shared, "Missouri provides very little state-level funding for education. As a percentage of total revenues only one other state (NH) provides less." They go on to state, "Funding in our region for education comes mostly from local sources (56%), followed by state sources (30%), followed by federal sources

Resources come in the form of time, talent, and financial dollars. And when we are using the time and talent of individuals, such as our parents, to serve in needed areas, we are saving financial dollars for areas that would otherwise be directed to hiring outsiders to provide the time and talent to address critical needs. Further, parents have greater insight and historical understanding of the schools where their children attend. And because of that, they often have a running start in understanding the nature of problems and the needs of the community, which is another savings that would otherwise be spent on outsiders, using that time to learn about the problem before being able to tackle it.

(7%). Local funding is inequitable; state funding is volatile; federal funding is restrictive. High-need districts disproportionately feel all of these shortcomings. The Foundation Formula is Missouri's way of determining how much state funding a district receives, and several aspects of it are inequitable by design" (Furtado et al., 2020).

Unfortunately, Missouri is not alone. These kinds of funding inequities exist in communities across the country. They perpetuate a system that already produces generational poverty in communities as underfunded, low performing schools produce even lower outcomes, further impacting the property values in the community, which then turn around and fund the schools. And the cycle continues. Figure 5.1 displays a comparison of academic performance in low-income students compared to higher-income students. The results clearly

FIGURE 5.1 NAEP National Proficiency Rates, Low-Income Students Compared to Higher-Income Students, 2019

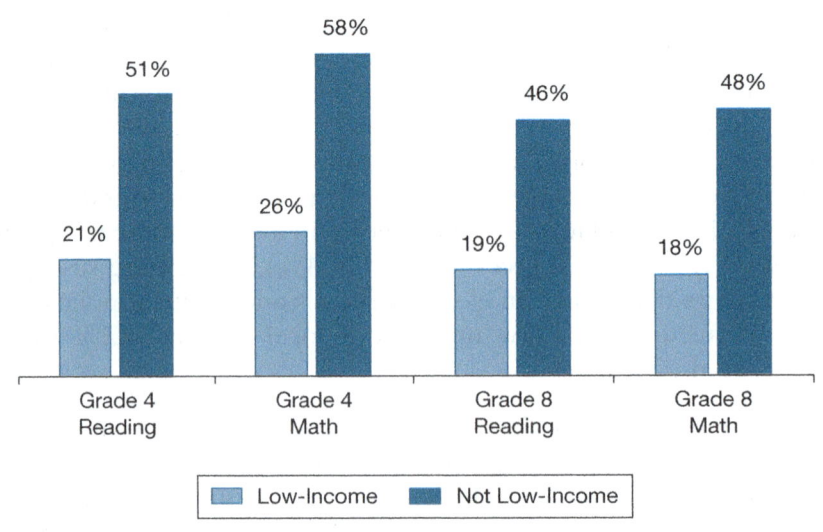

SOURCE: McKillip & Luhm, 2022, Educational Law Center.

BUILDING PARENT CAPACITY IN HIGH-POVERTY SCHOOLS

convey the urgency for leaders to close the gap by funding the needs of students who depend on public school.

To disrupt this cycle, leaders must work critically to understand their local, state, and government funding patterns/sources in order to decrease the disparities between communities. And although we can't necessarily change where the money comes from, we can be strategic with how we use it. Instead of thinking of funding from a deficit perspective, in which we never have enough, we need to shift our thinking to focus on how we use what we have and strategically look at the assets in the community, the staff, and across the school and district.

U: Use Funds Efficiently and Find Creative Sources

Ultimately, money is not the main barrier—the primary barrier is our own mindset. Unfortunately, when funding is viewed as a barrier, risk taking and innovation is limited and far too often the solution is generally to cut when you do not have enough. How we think about issues we face makes all the difference in our ability to problem solve and create and implement new solutions. While it is so easy to look first at what we do not have, we are challenged as educational leaders to reflect on what we do have and the capacity that does exist as a starting point.

Here are some ideas to use your funds more efficiently.

Consider investing in ways that can make your buildings more energy efficient and sustainable.

According to the US Department of Energy, across the nation schools spend more than $6 billion on energy each year. About 25 percent of that cost could be saved through smarter energy management, such as installing LED lighting and making sure that lights and computers are turned off at night and over weekends.

Stay on top of contract renewals.

Before automatically renewing contracts for regular services, such as cleaning, insurance, or landscaping, regularly review contracts early to ensure you are getting the best deal and have time to make adjustments within the terms. The same is true for online platforms and services. We are fortunate in Topeka to have an outstanding finance team that works closely with staff to review needs

> The Seattle School District saved $20,000 a year by turning off the lights in its 250 vending machines (US Department of Energy, 2002). The Capistrano Unified School District in Southern California began installing solar panels across the parking lots of all six of its high schools in 2019. At each school site, the system generates about 1.5 megawatts of power annually, which is enough to handle about 80 percent of their respective energy needs. The project was financed in bond sales. "The bonds will be paid off with the money the district will save on electricity costs . . . which is expected to be $849,000 a year, or $21 million over 25 years" (Nero, 2019).

and services. Make sure teachers and students are using the platform and services and that expected outcomes are being produced. Just because an online literacy platform is great, it doesn't mean you should renew the contract if only a small percentage of students and staff are actually using it.

Use school sites to raise funds.

Everyone loves to donate to a jog-a-thon or bake sale, but those types of fundraising methods place the burden on families to donate their own money. It just doesn't make sense to request donations from families who are already stretched thin, nor does it accomplish our goal of building up the community. Instead, think about how school sites can generate their own income (Kennedy, 2019). For example, can the school rent out space to local organizations that need a meeting location? Or perhaps sports fields can be rented to youth community sports leagues. School parking lots can even be rented out as paid parking for local events, if they're in the right location.

LIVED AND LEARNED

Think Creatively to Enable Cost Savings

▶ In Topeka, and in past districts, our leadership team members are tenacious with our budget and work hard to make sure we are good stewards of those funds. One way I enable cost savings is to strategically evaluate the roles and responsibilities throughout the district. Are there responsibilities that can be fulfilled through community partnerships or volunteers rather than district staff? Are there other responsibilities that can be covered with current internal staff rather than hiring additional staff?

To determine the types of opportunities that may exist, we take the time to ask staff about their strengths, interests, and ideas for continuous improvement. Through those discussions, new opportunities often develop that they can and want to help implement.

The savings generated from this kind of funding shift allows different needs to be addressed and can potentially lead to supplemental compensation in place of hiring additional staff for these opportunities. Ultimately, this positively impacts the quality of staff recruited and retained. Here are some examples of how this can practically play out.

Jennings School District, St. Louis

The director of human resources shared with me her interest in business and finance. This led us to provide training for her in federal programs, which resulted in her becoming our federal programs director alongside her human resources responsibilities. This one step allowed us to become more efficient with staffing and to better utilize resources within the district and improve our management of finances.

Our supervisor of safety was involved in after-school activities with youth and had an interest in helping students rebuild their lives after incarceration. This interest led to his oversight of our restorative justice program. As part of the program, students learned how to run the school's food pantry that they restocked as a small business. The program also included services for students who needed an alternative school setting after incarceration before returning to their neighborhood school.

I also functioned as the crossing guard every morning at a school next to the district office that needed a second crossing guard at a busy intersection, so that we didn't have to hire additional staff for that role. Not only did it save us money, but it also allowed me to be present in the community in authentic ways and talk to parents and children on a daily basis.

Topeka Public Schools, Topeka

When I started in Topeka in 2016, the district did not have an alternative school for students who were suspended or for students who were transitioning from incarceration but were not ready to return to a traditional school environment. There was not a fully functional virtual school, and there was not one person overseeing mental health partnerships. In assessing interests and experiences of staff, an exceptional school administrator, Dr. Joy Grimes, who had a background in counseling and alternative schools and was an assistant principal at one of the high schools, was selected to assist me with opening the first alternative school serving suspended middle- and high-school students. Through her role, oversight for virtual school, alternative school, the juvenile detention center, and mental health is now aligned, which allows our mental health and wraparound services to meet critical needs more efficiently.

We have also moved away from having multiple directors and offered the current practitioners the opportunity to be lead principals and part-time consulting teachers as leaders for their respective areas to mentor and develop colleagues while also serving in the same role. This allowed us to save resources by redistributing to the school and it empowered staff and built capacity within schools at the same time with job-embedded staff development daily.

D: Differentiate Between High-Priority Needs and Focus on Solutions

It's long been established that Maslow's hierarchy of basic needs—food, shelter, and safety—must be met before learning can take place. Therefore, when we target those family and student needs first, everything else changes. When I start leading anywhere, I begin by reviewing ways we use available resources to provide food, shelter, and security. In Virginia, this led to reorganizing the budget to hire full-time nurses at schools and providing greater access to meals, which immediately changed health access and outcomes for students and families. In Missouri, this meant funding before and after-school programs where dinner was also provided, which helped to ensure that students started the day ready to learn and left with full stomachs. And in Kansas, this meant partnering with local agencies to provide housing, food, and mental health services to families. The results and needs may be different across communities, but school and district leaders must always employ an innovative and creative approach to funding and partnerships in order to implement change and build parent capacity.

A mistake often made by new leaders especially, is to spread limited funds widely in order to address as many issues as possible. I refer to this as financing by fire—where leaders use funds for short-term, temporary solutions and quick fixes that are not sustainable for long-term success. In order to be successful, it is important to use a goal-focused approach that targets the highest-priority needs, with no more than about three to five areas of focus.

In order to determine the highest-priority needs, think back to what we discussed in Chapter 3—we cannot serve needs we do not know. Leaders have to put on their sneakers and walk their community, their schools, and their neighborhoods to meet people informally, learn about issues for themselves, and truly understand opportunities in the community. We must meet people where they are to walk alongside them and to lead them forward. This learning can then be combined with more formal needs assessments, such as surveys and questionnaires. As data is compiled and analyzed, patterns will emerge that will help inform the areas of highest priority and should be incorporated into strategic plans and goals for the year. The solution-oriented goals then become the priority areas to focus funding.

This type of solution-oriented planning must target the identified needs and include measurable outcomes to lead to the desired end goal. Plans that focus exclusively on tasks, such as hosting meetings, and not solutions will not change outcomes. Solution-oriented plans require gaining involvement from stakeholders across the district and community, leveraging partnerships to develop solutions that will address the problem. In solution-focused plans, creating accountability measures with dates by when specific benchmarks are to be completed helps ensure the targeted needs are met. As these priorities come to light and solution-oriented plans are put in place, keep these keys in mind:

1. **Listen to learn.** Identify assets and highest-priority needs/barriers to families being engaged in school.

2. **Avoid the distractions and temptations to serve widely** and focus on making deep concentrated change focused on specific needs.

3. **Develop a strategic plan** with goals, clear action steps, and a timeline to address the identified needs. This will help to keep you accountable.

If your school or district is ready to examine community needs and partnership planning more extensively, there are available tools for determining your School Health Index. According to the US Department of Health and Human Services (2017), the School Health Index is a self-assessment and planning guide that will enable school leaders to:

- "identify the strengths and weaknesses of your school's policies and programs for promoting health and safety

- develop an action plan for improving student health and safety

- involve teachers, parents, students, and the community in improving school policies, programs, and services"

When general funds are not available to meet identified high-priority needs, you need to look to community partners, grants, or other resources for support. The US Department of Education launched a new website under Secretary of Education Miguel Cardona that gives schools and parents tools to find grants and gain new resources. The website, https://www2.ed.gov/about/inits/list/index.html, provides information to access and apply for millions of dollars' worth of grants. It also provides capacity-building resources, such as links to webinars, articles, and more.

Resources and planning tools can be found here: https://www.cdc.gov/healthyschools/shi/

Fiscal mapping tools can also more extensively bring together community government and planning organizations and educational services to effect broad change. The use of these types of tools involves a collaborative partnership among many invested organizations, including potential nonprofit consultation services. The Forum for Youth Investment is one such organization. They provide tools and resources here: https://forumfyi.org/fiscal-mapping-tools/

 **LIVED AND LEARNED**

People First, Not Resources

▶ When you identify a need or barrier, if you start by talking about resources first, the answer is almost always no. Can we do this? No, we don't have money. But how you serve the most vulnerable says a lot about who you are. So, I never want to start a conversation about filling a need or building parent capacity by discussing resources first. Our Jennings Hope House is a good example of this.

(Continued)

(Continued)

In Jennings School District in 2015, we had a significant number of homeless youth, especially unaccompanied youth (homeless children under the age of twenty-one without physical custody of a parent or guardian). Those children did not have parents or family members around or had parents without the capacity to care for their children—perhaps as a result of death, incarceration, or mental illness—so our school family had the responsibility to step in to give those children what they needed to be successful.

We were trying to figure out ways to support this population of students and I had heard about a creative solution that a neighboring district had implemented, so I took a team to go check it out. Maplewood Richmond Heights School District had purchased a home, which they called Joe's Place, through grants and private donations. In collaboration with Crossroads Presbyterian Fellowship Church, they turned the home into a foster house for homeless unaccompanied youth and hired two house parents to run it. It was a quick success and was providing the kind of structure and support I knew we needed for our students in Jennings.

We were so inspired that we immediately collaborated with our district facilities department to see if we owned any buildings or homes that we could turn into our own version of Joe's Place. Sure enough, we owned a vacant home and so we got to work flipping it right away. I told the team that we had thirty days to get it ready for students to move in, just like those shows on HGTV. They thought I was crazy, but to me, every day we didn't work on this project was another day that a child went homeless without the necessary tools for stability and success in their life. Now that we had a solution that could work, we didn't have any more time to waste!

We used available local and donated funds and established a 501(c)(3) for the district to be able to accept private donations and support needs long-term across the district. As we worked, local media began publicizing our story and more and more private donations came flooding in. Many people from construction businesses around the city, and even our own facilities crews, donated materials, as well as their time and talent to working on the renovation. As we got the house ready for students and the two house parents we hired to run the house, we knew we needed furniture and decorations to make it a livable and functional space. So, we cut pictures out of magazines to make signs describing what we needed and taped them up all around the house—there was a sign for a couch taped to the wall of the living room, a sign for a table and chairs in the dining room, an extra-large refrigerator in the kitchen, beds in each of the bedrooms, there were signs everywhere! Whenever someone asked how they could help or went on a tour to see what was going on in the house, people would see the signs, take one off the wall, and then bring back that item. The generosity of the community and local businesses was incredible. We were able to furnish the whole house from the goodness of other people.

In later years, Jennings School District actually owns and operates two Hope Houses—one for boys and one for girls—and they were both very successful and made such a difference in the lives of the students who live there.

G: Garner Support by Telling Stories Well

Schools are the center of the community. What happens in the schools impacts the community, and what occurs in the community directly impacts the school. This is why partnerships in the community are essential. The entire community must own and invest in solutions from a grassroots level, and school leaders are especially equipped to create pathways for those opportunities. This is why mindset is critical.

Garnering support begins with identifying partners and agencies that are also spending funds on needs in the community. This can include social service agencies, food banks, grocery stores, businesses, nonprofit organizations, or even individuals who live in the community. As we identify potential partners, it's important to paint the picture of who you are and why the service or need is important for the success of the school, the students, and families. I never begin a conversation with a list of what they can do for us or what we can do for them. I begin with how we can work together to improve our community. By telling our story well, we are able to focus on ways we can collaborate, needs we can address, and assets we both have to build from. As a result, grants are secured, volunteers are identified for tutoring services or mentoring, financial investments are started from philanthropic investors, and we identify ways we can collaborate to extending resources through joint efforts.

LIVED AND LEARNED

Share the Story to Bring Clarity and Purpose to the Investment

▶ When I first started as superintendent in Topeka, many residents spoke up about the disparities on the east side of the community. They felt that residents in other areas of the community were not invested. This deficit thinking prevented those in the district from creating a visionary plan to gain investments from the broader community. So, the deputy superintendent and I shared the story of our schools and wrote an action plan focused on investment in three critical areas and presented it to Advisors Excel, a large financial firm in the community. The critical areas included college and career readiness, building relationships, and capacity-building investments. The plan outlined funding engagement opportunities with clear action steps that would build relationships with parents, teachers, and students, and demonstrated how an investment in three schools that are feeders to East Topeka High School could result in increased academic gains for students and improved outcomes for families. It provided ways that funding could help facilitate relationship

(Continued)

(Continued)

building between parents and schools and invest in needed resources for teachers and schools, including supplies and supporting curriculum needs. It also included funding opportunities that would provide college course offerings for students, mentoring, and field trip opportunities. Advisors Excel invested in the plan, and eight years later, despite principal changes at the feeder schools, the system remained and the graduation rates at East Topeka High School have improved by 20 percentage points (from a 60 percent graduation rate to more than an 80 percent graduation rate). Overall, the community health rankings and outcomes, as measured by the Shawnee County Health Department, began to improve. The homeless student population decreased by more than 200, and the health map provided by the city of Topeka indicating healthy neighborhoods based on crime and poverty started to show an increase in healthy neighborhoods.

FIGURE 5.2   Health Index Map Topeka, KS 2020

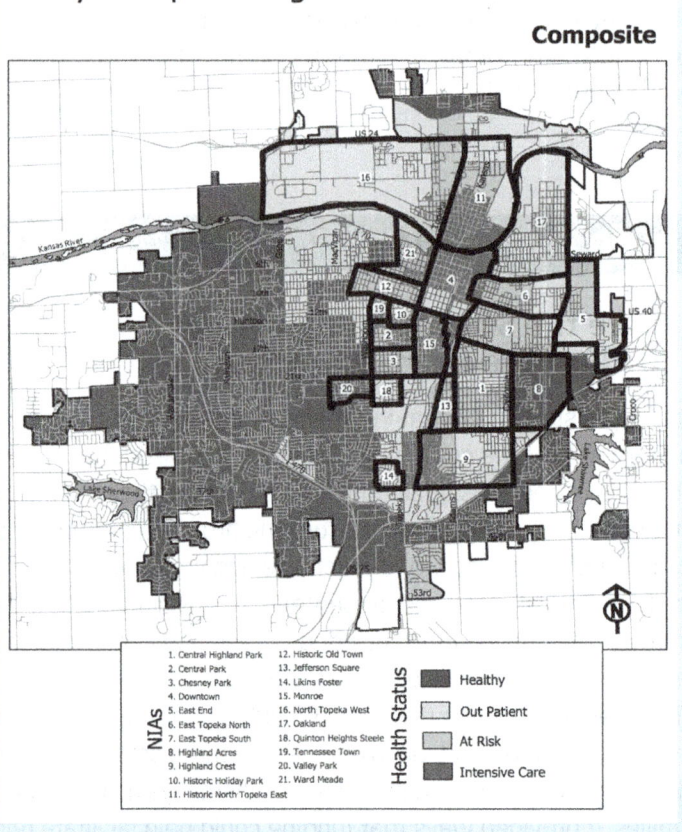

SOURCE: https://cot-wp-uploads.s3.amazonaws.com/wp-content/uploads/planning/NHoodHealthUpdate2020/Composite Map.pdf

E: Empower and Educate Families on School Funding

It's important to build capacity around school funding in order to truly expect parents and educators to be knowledgeable and act as school co-creators. Funds are generally spent in four main areas. Those areas include:

- **General Fund:** The general fund is the main operating fund for the school district. A district may have only one general fund.

- **Special Revenue:** These funds come from specific revenue sources and are legally restricted or committed for specific purposes, as specified from the sources of the money. An example would be state or federal grants.

- **Debt Service Fund:** This is money specifically assigned to pay off principal and interest related to debt that the district owes.

- **Capital Projects Fund:** Capital projects funds are financial resources that are restricted, committed, or assigned to expenses related to building, maintaining, or acquiring buildings and other facilities.

The best way for parents to understand how their school and district spends money is to participate in the decision-making process by attending the main places where public education spending decisions are made (Wilde, 2023). These include:

- PTA or PTO meetings

- School site council meetings

- School board meetings

- State government budgeting sessions

Think about your first years as a teacher (or an administrator). It's likely you spent a significant amount of time just learning education-specific jargon and acronyms. School finance can also feel like that for parents and community members, so it is helpful to provide them with a glossary of terms (see Figure 5.3) to help make the world of finance simpler. You can even provide finance workshops, focusing on topics such as budgeting, effective meal planning on a budget, and college savings. "The world of school finance is a complex, ever-shifting landscape. Knowing a few basic terms can be a big advantage to parents choosing a school and making their way through the public school system" (Wilde, 2023).

FIGURE 5.3 Parent Glossary of School Financial Terms

Glossary of School Financial Terms

Categorical funds: Restricted school district funds given to schools that can only be spent on specified programs.

Charter schools: Public schools that have flexibility in structuring academic programs, hiring teachers, and carrying out other functions. The degree of freedom that charter schools have differs by state. These are generally funded by a combination of public and private funds.

ESSA: On December 10, 2015, President Barack Obama signed the Every Student Succeeds Act (ESSA), reauthorizing the federal Elementary and Secondary Education Act (ESEA) and replacing the No Child Left Behind Act (NCLB), the 2001 reauthorization of ESEA. The ESSA took effect beginning in the 2017–2018 school year. ESSA (formerly NCLB) increases the federal government's role in assessing student achievement and further restricts the allocation of federal funds accordingly.

Free/reduced price lunch program: A federal program for students whose families fall below the federal poverty line. The number of students at a school that qualify for this program is frequently used as a measure of the school's socioeconomic demographic makeup.

General fund: Unrestricted money in school district budgets given to schools for general educational purposes.

Parcel taxes: Voter-approved assessments on parcels of property that are used for general education purposes (as opposed to school facilities, which is what bonds pay for).

Property taxes: Taxes on local properties—this makes up a large part of a school district's budget.

School bonds: Voter-approved loans that are used to pay for school facilities.

School district foundations: Private nonprofit groups that administer grants to school districts to help pay for "extras," and, in some cases, more substantial programs, such as music and libraries, that school districts would otherwise have to cut.

State lotteries: Many states use these revenues to supplement public education funding. Often this source of funding represents only a small percentage of lottery profits and is not a stable source of funding for schools.

Titles I–X: Ten sections of NCLB. Perhaps the most well-known is Title 1, which provides funds for students from low-income families.

SOURCE: Terms and definitions from Wilde, 2023.

Gain Trust Through Simplicity and Transparency

► When I led the Jennings School District, rather than providing complex graphs to educate the public, we provided three simple PowerPoint slides. The first slide showed the overall funds in each of our four main categories of spending (general fund, special revenue, debt service fund, and capital projects fund). The other two slides showed the increases and decreases in each type of fund. With this approach, the board and community members had enough understanding to ask critical questions and to further advocate for school funding. As a result of this capacity-building focus, the district ultimately established its own not-for-profit fund, which opened the opportunity for community partners/donors to directly contribute monetary donations to it, which made it easier and more feasible to fund established critical needs in the district without affecting the overall district budget.

If nothing else, empower your parents to understand that every district bond passed is passed by the vote of families. Every politician and school board member elected into office got there because of votes from parents in the community. Parents have power that, when leveraged, can change the course of education. We have seen this demonstrated through the courageous parents involved as plaintiffs in the *Brown v. Board of Education* case and in countless other communities since.

T: Train and Retain High-Quality Educators

National Public Radio interviewed Linda Darling-Hammond at Stanford University who shared, "A marginal dollar spent to get more highly qualified teachers produces more gains in achievement than almost any other marginal use of that dollar" (Lloyd, 2016). While many struggle with understanding the correlation between school funding and teacher quality, we can learn from looking further at what is working around us in districts like Massachusetts. According to a 2022 report, Massachusetts has the highest teacher salaries in the country. It is no surprise they also have high student outcomes relative to districts of similar size in

In addition to using funds to retain high-quality teachers and educators, you can use your budget to recycle economic dollars into the community by filling open classified staff or paraprofessional jobs with parents from your community. When parents are employed, they are better able to provide for their families and student outcomes improve. In Topeka Public Schools, at least 10 percent of our staff is made up of parents. If you are unable to hire parents, connect them with other job opportunities, career fairs, and social services.

other states. In many reports, Massachusetts has ranked higher than many other large urban schools systems in performance and "almost half of all Massachusetts public schools are in the top 25 percent of public schools in the country, according to a recent ranking by U.S. News and World Report" (Martin, 2022). The correlation between teacher salary and school outcomes is significant, and is one of many factors impacted by school funding.

HOPE FOR THE FUTURE

While funding systems are difficult to change through the legislature and the foundation formula may set parameters that restrict funding that are beyond the control of the school leader, there is hope. School leaders and school boards determine the priorities and the spending habits that can make a difference in parent and student outcomes. There's also hope in legislative advocacy to change the outdated foundation formula systems impacting countless students in states across the country. Any change starts with a hopeful outlook in viewing what's possible.

Ultimately, when we fund schools well, we are funding a promise for a better future. Opportunity gaps do not close on their own; they close with the help of many people working together to fill the gaps and create a bridge to provide greater opportunities.

FINANCING YOUR VISION IN ACTION

As a 2016 *EdWeek* Leaders to Learn From recipient, I have met countless Leaders to Learn From and have since used the *EdWeek* initiative as a personal resource to identify new visionary school leaders to learn from on my own leadership journey. Recently, I learned about Cyndi Tercero-Sandavol, the family and community engagement manager at Phoenix Union High School District in Phoenix, Arizona. As an administrator, she understands that in many situations, money is power. Her vision is to share some of that power by giving parents and students a voice in how certain funds are spent within the district. Cyndi refers to this approach as participatory budgeting, where she provides a budget to students and parents to identify ways to support their own key needs, which has empowered them to change outcomes in their own school settings.

Cyndi grew up in poverty, which created many struggles for her, but also gave fuel to her purpose-filled vision of expanding opportunities for students and families giving voice into how money is spent in the district. As part of the participatory budgeting process, Cyndi provides opportunities for parents and students to share their ideas through forums and focus groups. A recent budget discussion has centered on what to do with the district's public safety funds. These funds became available as a result of cancelling their school resource officers' contract through the local police department in the aftermath of the police killing of George Floyd. Cyndi shared with EdWeek, "During one of the public forums, a parent said her biggest concern about her son's safety was whether she could muster the funds to pay for athletics. She was afraid he would be bullied for being too poor to buy the right clothes and equipment" (Lieberman, 2023). As a result of that parent's voice, sports fees were abolished at schools. Without participatory budgeting, Cyndi acknowledged that this conversation would never have happened. By thinking creatively and empowering key stakeholders (parents and students) through voice and choice, Cyndi's vision for shared ownership of school/district budgeting is transforming family and student engagement in Phoenix, Arizona.

FINANCING YOUR VISION REFLECTION

Think back to what you read throughout this chapter. Use these reflection questions to consider your own school or district and the role you play in building parent capacity.

1. Think about the acronym BUDGET. Which letter impacted your thinking about school funding the most and why?

2. What high-priority needs are not funded well in your school or district and what do you think could be done to change that?

3. Through your role as school or district leader, what steps can you take to advocate, bring awareness about, and change spending and funding habits?

Take some time to reflect on your learning and plan for action in your next steps.

WHAT?

Summarize your learning and key takeaways from this chapter.

SO WHAT?

Record ideas about how your key takeaways apply to you, your school, and/or your district.

NOW WHAT?

Based on your key takeaways, plan your next steps for moving forward in this area.

Conclusion

Inspired by Linda Brown and a Call to Action

Education is a civil right—not just for some; for all children. But it is a right that can only be realized with the advocacy and engagement of parents. The Civil Rights Movement paralleled what was occurring in education in schools in Topeka, Kansas, in 1954, in Little Rock, Arkansas, in 1957, and in states across the country that were being integrated as a result of parents who wanted their children to have access to the resources within their neighborhoods. The collective voice of that small group of parents in Topeka changed the nation. Those parents created a bridge for others they would never meet, and there is still more to do in order to build the capacity of parents to have the access and opportunities all students deserve. Although we have come a long way, the realities of today's education system show us that we still have a long way to go. Our destinies, and those of our children, are intertwined with the demands of those who came before us.

Shortly after being announced as the superintendent of Topeka Public Schools in 2016, I attended a service at St. Mark's AME Church in North Topeka, where Rev. Oliver Brown (Linda Brown's father) served as pastor during the 1950s. After the service, the first person I met was the organ player, Ms. Linda Brown-Thompson. I was in awe to actually meet someone so pivotal to my life's trajectory and to the lives of so many like me; but to those in the church she was simply Linda Brown.

Her quiet demeanor was unassuming, but anyone around her knew she was a force to be reckoned with. And I will never forget the words she said to me. She told me that she and her grandchildren who attended school in Topeka expected great things from me. She also said that the community had waited a long time, having paved the way for me more than sixty years ago. She died in 2018, just two years after I met her.

As leaders, parents, and community members, our children are counting on us and they expect great things, and we shouldn't keep them waiting any longer. With the urgency our children's education demands, use the tools gained in this book as a resource to add to your momentum in building parent capacity in schools. Those who came before us gave us all a running start so that we could take the baton and run our race, creating a new path for those who follow.

Appendices

Appendix A

School Climate Survey

SCHOOL CLIMATE SURVEY

Dear Families,

We want our school to be the best it can be. Please complete this survey and tell us what you think are the school's strong points and where we can improve. Your honest comments and ideas are very welcome. If you would like to help tally and analyze the results, please let us know.

The Family and Community Involvement Action Team

No	SCHOOL ENVIRONMENT
1	The people make me feel welcome when I walk into this school. ○ Always ○ Almost Always ○ Sometimes ○ Rarely ○ Never
2	The school environment makes me feel welcome when I walk into this school. ○ Always ○ Almost Always ○ Sometimes ○ Rarely ○ Never
3	I am treated with respect at the school. ○ Always ○ Almost Always ○ Sometimes ○ Rarely ○ Never
4	I see my cultural heritage reflected in aspects of the building/campus itself. ○ Always ○ Almost Always ○ Sometimes ○ Rarely ○ Never
5	Students at the school are treated fairly no matter what their race or cultural background. ○ Always ○ Almost Always ○ Sometimes ○ Rarely ○ Never
6	I feel welcome at school-related activities or functions. ○ Always ○ Almost Always ○ Sometimes ○ Rarely ○ Never

No	PROBLEM SOLVING
7	I have a good working relationship with my child/children's teacher(s). ○ Always ○ Almost Always ○ Sometimes ○ Rarely ○ Never
8	I can talk to the school principal or other administrators when I need to. ○ Always ○ Almost Always ○ Sometimes ○ Rarely ○ Never
9	I know who to go to when I have specific questions. ○ Always ○ Almost Always ○ Sometimes ○ Rarely ○ Never

No	PROBLEM SOLVING (CONT.)
10	**The school has a clear process for addressing my concerns.** ○ Always ○ Almost Always ○ Sometimes ○ Rarely ○ Never
11	**If the school can't help me, I know they will refer me to someone who can.** ○ Always ○ Almost Always ○ Sometimes ○ Rarely ○ Never
12	**I feel welcomed and encouraged to make suggestions for improvement or share new ideas.** ○ Always ○ Almost Always ○ Sometimes ○ Rarely ○ Never

No	COMMUNICATION
13	**I feel informed about available resources at school.** ○ Always ○ Almost Always ○ Sometimes ○ Rarely ○ Never
14	**I feel informed about events and activities happening at school.** ○ Always ○ Almost Always ○ Sometimes ○ Rarely ○ Never
15	**I feel informed about ways to get involved/volunteer at school.** ○ Always ○ Almost Always ○ Sometimes ○ Rarely ○ Never
16	**A translator is available easily, if needed.** ○ Always ○ Almost Always ○ Sometimes ○ Rarely ○ Never
17	**Communication is regular and timely.** ○ Always ○ Almost Always ○ Sometimes ○ Rarely ○ Never
18	**Staff at the school consult me and other families before making important decisions.** ○ Always ○ Almost Always ○ Sometimes ○ Rarely ○ Never
19	**I understand the school rules and expectations around student behavior, academics, and dress.** ○ Always ○ Almost Always ○ Sometimes ○ Rarely ○ Never

(Continued)

(Continued)

No	SATISFACTION
20	**I am satisfied with the quality of the school.** ◯ Always ◯ Almost Always ◯ Sometimes ◯ Rarely ◯ Never
21	**I would recommend this school to other families and friends.** ◯ Always ◯ Almost Always ◯ Sometimes ◯ Rarely ◯ Never

No	OPEN RESPONSE
22	**What is the school doing that is most helpful to you as a parent?**
23	**What changes would you like to see at the school?**

Thank you for your participation!

Please return this survey to:

Appendix B
Conference Checklist

BEFORE THE CONFERENCE

1. **Notify parents about the following:**
   - Purpose
   - Time and location options
   - Length of time
   - Childcare or transportation options

2. **Prepare:**
   - Gather official necessary documents (report card, progress report, etc.)
   - Gather student work samples
   - Gather other materials (observational checklists/rubrics, anecdotal notes, etc.)
   - Gather input from student (if appropriate)
   - Schedule additional conference participants, if appropriate (translator, administrator, etc.)
   - Plan what to say and questions to ask (avoid specialized educational terms)

3. **Plan agenda:**
   - Create plan for the flow of the conference
   - Emphasize cooperation (what can we do together?)

4. **Arrange environment:**
   - Place seating away from desk
   - Make sure seating space is clear from clutter or other school materials

- Make sure all materials are easily accessible and easily seen/discussed together
- Make sure there is privacy
- Make sure room feels welcoming and inviting

DURING THE CONFERENCE

1. **Welcome.** Establish rapport and open opportunity to share.

2. **Set terms.** State the purpose of the conference, remind of time limits, encourage note taking and questions, and mention options for follow-up after the conference.

3. **Lead with the positive.** Share the child's major strengths, both academic and social. Share what you enjoy most and what makes the child unique.

4. **Open the floor.** Ask parents to share any comments, information, or observations they see or ask any initial questions.

5. **Show.** Share evidence of the child's academic and/or social growth.

6. **Listen.** Ask for feedback from parents. Look for verbal and nonverbal clues about how things are going and invite additional questions.

7. **Share opportunities for growth and develop an action plan.** Share areas for academic or social growth. Be specific. Develop an action plan focusing on one or two areas with action items for both parents and teacher(s).

8. **Summarize.** Summarize the conversation and plan next meeting time to check in on action plan.

9. **End with the positive.** Express confidence in the child's ability to meet goals and continue growth. Share excitement and appreciation for parent-teacher partnership to support child's growth.

AFTER THE CONFERENCE

1. **Review** the action plan and make sure you strategically integrate agreed-on steps into instruction.

2. **Share** action plan information with other school staff, resource teachers, etc., if needed, especially if other teachers support the child outside your classroom.

3. **Send** a follow-up thank you note or email to the parents.

4. **Mark calendar** with the planned follow-up date/timeline.

Appendix C

Vision in Action Template

VISION IN ACTION	
Value	How do we demonstrate this value with each other?
Value	How do we demonstrate this value with families and the community?

(Continued)

(Continued)

VISION IN ACTION	
Value	How do we demonstrate this value with students?

Appendix D

Vision in Action

Action Plan

GOAL:

KEY ACTIVITIES	BY WHOM	BY WHEN

WHAT RESOURCES DO YOU *HAVE* TO SUPPORT THE EXECUTION OF THESE ACTIONS?

WHAT RESOURCES DO YOU *NEED* TO SUPPORT THE EXECUTION OF THESE ACTIONS?

(Continued)

(Continued)

IDENTIFY ANY ADDITIONAL EXPENSES ASSOCIATED WITH THESE ACTIONS AS WELL AS POTENTIAL FUNDING SOURCES.		
ASSOCIATED EXPENSE	TYPE OF EXPENSE (ONE TIME, SHORT-TERM, ONGOING)	POTENTIAL FUNDING SOURCE

WHAT ADDITIONAL SUPPORT OR OUTSIDE INVOLVEMENT DO YOU NEED TO SUPPORT THE EXECUTION OF THESE ACTIONS? (e.g., new community partner, outside consultant, district leader)

HOW WILL YOU MONITOR PROGRESS FOR EACH OF THE IDENTIFIED ACTIONS? WHAT DOES SUCCESS LOOK LIKE?

Appendix E

Resources for Families

HOUSING AND SOCIAL SERVICES

EconEdLink provides grades K–12 economics and personal finance resources, including high-quality lesson plans, videos, assessments, activities, professional development webinars, and more for educators. EconEdLink was created by the Council for Economic Education, which delivers economic and financial education to students from kindergarten through high school. https://econedlink.org/

Feed the Children is a leading hunger relief organization. In addition to providing food to children in nearly all fifty states, Feed the Children also provides essential items like shampoo, soap, toothpaste, and cleaning products. There are five distribution centers in the United States, which allows the organization to deliver resources to communities in cities and rural areas to help families thrive. They also provide summer meal support and have an interactive map that families can use to find local food distribution centers during the summer months when the children are not in school. https://www.feedthechildren.org/get-involved/campaigns/summer-hunger/summer-meals/

Feeding America is the largest charity working to end hunger in the United States. It is part of a nationwide network of food banks, food pantries, and community-based organizations that focus on ending hunger. They also provide a vast set of resources to support feeding children and families, including the ability to search their network for resources in your local area as well as how to start a food pantry in your school or district. https://www.feedingamerica.org/our-work/hunger-relief-programs

First Book Marketplace is a website where educators can shop for new books at steep discounts—typically 50 percent to 90 percent off. To qualify, the school must have a student population where 70 percent or more qualify for free or reduced lunch. https://www.fbmarketplace.org

Funders for Housing and Opportunity (FHO) is a nationwide funder collaborative committed to improving stable housing options, especially for those who have historically been underserved or denied access. FHO has awarded nearly $23 million in grants across the county to support fair and equitable housing opportunities. Organizations can apply for grants by invitation or a formal RFP processes. https://www.housingisopportunity.org

Half Price Books is the largest family-owned retailer for new and used books, with more than 100 stores nationwide. Half Price Books accepts donation requests from certain 501(c)(3) nonprofit organizations and educators, but can only fulfill requests in the areas where they currently operate. https://www.hpb.com

KidsNeedtoRead.org provides books, periodicals, and literacy resources to schools, libraries, and other organizations that administer literacy programs to disadvantaged children and adolescents. At least 50 percent of the children served by these organizations must be living at or below the national poverty rate. An application must be submitted in order to receive books. https://www.kidsneedtoread.org

Mobile Health Map is a database of mobile clinics in the United States (more than 3,000 nationwide). Members of this collaborative network supply information about their location, services, target populations, and costs. Their website can be used to find and schedule a mobile clinic at your school site. https://www.mobilehealthmap.org/find-clinics/

National Center for Homeless Education has a helpful brief for homeless service providers and homeless education staff to help them understand their roles in supporting youth and families experiencing homelessness, while offering tools and strategies to enhance collaboration among agencies. The brief is found here: https://nche.ed.gov/wp-content/uploads/2018/10/hud.pdf

TECHNOLOGY

Affordable Connectivity Program is a federally funded program that provides a $30 discount on monthly internet bills for qualifying households. Among the qualifications, families whose children are enrolled for free or reduced lunch can receive the benefit. Unfortunately, only about 25 percent of eligible households that qualify are even enrolled. A resource for school districts called the Affordable Connectivity Program Adoption Toolkit can be found at EducationSuperHighway.org.

MobileCitizen.org is a nonprofit that provides low-cost mobile internet with unlimited data plans exclusively to nonprofit organizations, educational entities, libraries, and social welfare agencies. Through partnership with this organization and coordination with other qualifying agencies in your community, you could bring internet access to students and their families throughout many locations in your community. http://www.mobilecitizen.org

T-Mobile Project 10Million is run in partnership with Boys and Girls Club of America and T-Mobile, and is committed to connecting students in Grades K–12 with Wi-Fi and data. Families, schools, or entire districts can apply. Each qualifying household receives a free hotspot with 100GB of data per year for five years. https://www.t-mobile.com/brand/project-10-million

TalkingPoints is an education technology nonprofit that works to increase student success by using technology to enhance family engagement in their child's education. Through its app-based service, parents and educators use human and AI-powered, two-way translation in order to communicate in approximately 150 different languages. https://talkingpts.org

GRANTS AND FUNDING OPPORTUNITIES

Carnegie Corporation of New York funds programs that seek to establish better partnerships between home and school and make sure families know how to best support their children's education and act as advocates for change. You can apply for grants on their web page. https://www.carnegie.org

Community Services Block Grant is a federally funded grant that provides funds to states, territories, and tribes to administer to support services that alleviate the causes and conditions of poverty in under resourced communities. Grants are funded for services and activities including housing, nutrition, utility, and transportation assistance; and employment, education, and other income- and asset-building services. https://www.acf.hhs.gov/ocs/programs/community-services-block-grant-csbg

HundrEd is a global network of members who look for impactful and scalable education innovations, and help education providers, such as schools or districts, implement their ideas. Once HundrED finds a project to implement, they work to equip educational systems with the structure, frameworks, processes, and capacity required to successfully adapt and implement the idea or program. https://hundred.org

State Interagency Councils on Homelessness consist of cross-system member organizations to coordinate the homelessness strategy for their regions or states. They offer assistance to local leaders and providers, including educational agencies and boards of education. https://usich.gov/local-assistance/state-interagency-councils

Statewide Family Engagement Centers Program provides grants to organizations that offer technical assistance and training to state and local educational agencies as they seek to implement or improve their family engagement programs and policies with the aim of enhancing student development and academic achievement. https://oese.ed.gov/offices/office-of-discretionary-grants-support-services/school-choice-improvement-programs/statewide-family-engagement-centers-program/

AGENCIES, NETWORKS, AND RESOURCES

Equity Assistance Centers are funded by the US Department of Education to give school districts help in the areas of race, gender, national origin, and religion to ensure equal education opportunities for all. https://oese.ed.gov/offices/office-of-formula-grants/program-and-grantee-support-services/training-and-advisory-services-equity-assistance-centers/

Forum for Youth Investment provides fiscal mapping tools to help bring together community government/planning organizations and educational services to affect broad change. The use of these types of tools involves a collaborative partnership among many invested organizations, including potential nonprofit consultation services. https://forumfyi.org/fiscal-mapping-tools/

National Alliance for Family Engagement provides resources and training to help educators and community members communicate effectively. Free resources are available through their website. https://famengage.org/

National Alliance on Mental Illness (NAMI) is a national program focused on mental health. Most cities have a NAMI organization that can provide free resources and training. One way they do this is through their Parents & Teachers as Allies program, which is an in-service training focused on helping school professionals and families better understand mental illness early warning signs among youth. https://www.nami.org

National Association for Family, School, and Community Engagement provides resources and support to give you the ideas and tools you need to enhance and improve your school or district's practices in the area of family engagement. Many resources are free, but additional resources are offered for members such as webinars, networking, and in-person conventions. https://nafsce.org

National PTA has a website that includes a variety of tools to help support parent engagement, including family resources, parent guides and toolkits, and assessments/standards to help you identify areas of growth within your school or district. https://www.pta.org

National Schools of Character consists of educators, researchers, business and civic leaders who care deeply about the vital role that character will play in our future. Character.org helps schools create a "family" culture that works together toward shared values that guide behaviors in the school, home, and community. https://character.org

Parent Teacher Home Visits seeks to quip educators with the training needed to develop trusting relationships with families in service of student success and school improvement. Customized, interactive, and dynamic sessions give teachers a better understanding of and respect for families and the role they play as their child's first educators. Through the trainings, educators learn how to build trust with families and better engage students. https://pthvp.org

Parents as Teachers (**PAT**) is a national, evidence-based program focused on empowering parents by partnering with them to build strong communities, thriving families, and children who are healthy and ready for school. PAT provides free services to families with children prenatal through kindergarten, and PAT staff support, teach, and connect with families to help them understand and build their role as a child's first educator. https://parentsas-teachers.org

School Health Index Self-Assessment and Planning Guide is an evaluation and planning tool based on the CDC's guidelines for establishing school health programs most likely to help reduce health risk behaviors among youth. https://www.cdc.gov/healthyschools/shi/

School-Based Health Alliance is a nonprofit that advocates for high-quality health care in schools for the nation's most vulnerable children. They also provide services to help support community and school partnerships that establish new school-based health centers or assess those already in existence. https://www.sbh4all.org

United States Department of Education is a resource with grants and programs for family engagement, and also has information for high-poverty school districts and communities. https://www2.ed.gov/about/inits/list/index.html

United Way provides support to communities through grants that address the social determinants of health. https://www.unitedway.org/

References

Allegretto, S., García, E., & Weiss, E. (2022). *Public education funding in the U.S. needs an overhaul: How a larger federal role would boost equity and shield children from disinvestment during downturns*. Economic Policy Institute. https://www.epi.org/publication/public-education-funding-in-the-us-needs-an-overhaul/

Allington, R., & McGill-Franzen, A. (2009). Comprehension difficulties among struggling readers. In S. E. Israel & G. G. Duffy (Eds.), *Handbook of research on reading comprehension* (1st ed.). Routledge. https://doi.org/10.4324/9781315759609

Anderson, T. (2016). Remembering Rodney McAllister: Youth killed by stray dogs in 2001 would be 25. *The St. Louis American*. https://www.stlamerican.com/news/local_news/remembering-rodney-mcallister-youth-killed-by-stray-dogs-in-2001-would-be-25/article_f20987ca-e6e3-11e5-91e1-3f6e19874b02.html

Annie E. Casey Foundation. (2020). *Prioritizing housing security for young people and families during the pandemic*. https://www.aecf.org/blog/prioritizing-housing-security-for-young-people-and-families-during-the-pand

Aristotle. (1925). *Nichomachean ethics: Book II* (W. D. Ross, Trans.). The Internet Classics Archive. (Original work published 350 BCE) http://classics.mit.edu/Aristotle/nicomachaen.2.ii.html

Attendance Works. (2018). *Chronic absenteeism: 10 facts about school attendance*. https://www.attendanceworks.org/chronic-absence/the-problem/10-facts-about-school-attendance/

Auerbach, S. (2010). Beyond coffee with the principal: Toward leadership for authentic school-family partnerships. *Journal of School Leadership, 20*, 728–757.

Bahr, S., Sparks, D., & Hoyer, K. M. (2018). *Why didn't students complete a free application for federal student aid (FAFSA)? A detailed look*. National Center for Education Statistics. https://files.eric.ed.gov/fulltext/ED590789.pdf

Baker, T. L., Wise, J., Kelley, G., & Skiba, R. J. (2016). Identifying barriers: Creating solutions to improve family engagement. *School Community Journal, 26*(2), 161–184.

Bandura, A. (1994). *Self-efficacy*. https://www.wellcoach.com/memberships/images/Self-Efficacy1.pdf

Boykin, A. W., & Noguera, P. (2011). *Creating the opportunity to learn: Moving from research to practice to close the achievement gap*. ASCD.

Burga, S. (2021). How a mobile DMV could serve New Jersey's most vulnerable populations. *Next City News*. https://nextcity.org/urbanist-news/how-a-mobile-dmv-could-serve-new-jerseys-most-vulnerable-populations

Burtless, G. (1996). *Does money matter? The effect of school resources on student achievement and adult success* (Dialogues on Public Policy). Brookings Institution Press.

Centers for Disease Control and Prevention. (2019). *Parent engagement for school districts and school administrators*. https://www.cdc.gov/healthyyouth/protective/factsheets/parentengagement_administrators.htm

Centers for Disease Control and Prevention. (2022). *New CDC data illuminate youth mental health threats during the COVID-19 pandemic.* https://www.cdc.gov/media/releases/2022/p0331-youth-mental-health-covid-19.html

Chakraborty, B. (2022). *Medical deserts: What they are, where they are, and who they affect.* Washington Examiner. https://www.washingtonexaminer.com/policy/healthcare/medical-deserts-what-where-explained

Childress, S. (2012). Do you live in a "Dental Desert"? Check our map. *Frontline News.* https://www.pbs.org/wgbh/frontline/article/do-you-live-in-a-dental-desert-check-our-map/

Communities in Schools. (2023). *Collaboration conversation: How partnerships create school-wide impact at Title-1 schools.* https://www.communitiesinschools.org/articles/article/collaboration-conversation-how-partnerships-create-school-wide-impact-at-title-i-schools/

Covey, S. (1989). *The 7 habits of highly effective people.* Simon and Schuster.

Delgado-Gaitan, C. (2001). *The power of community: Mobilizing for family and schooling.* Rowman and Littlefield.

DeWitt, P. (2017). *School climate: Leading with collective efficacy.* Corwin.

DeWitt, P. (2019). How collective teacher efficacy develops. *Educational Leadership, 76,* 31–35.

DeWitt, P., & Slade, S. (2014). *School climate change: How do I build a positive environment for learning?* ASCD.

Donne, J. *For whom the bell tolls.* (n.d./1624). www.yourdailypoem.com/listpoem.jsp?poem_id=2118

Education Law Center. (2020). *Making the grade 2020: How fair is school funding in your state?* https://edlawcenter.org/research/making-the-grade-2020.html

Educational Leadership. (2012). *Feedback for learning* (Vol. 70, No. 1). ASCD.

Epstein, J. L. (2001). Effects on student achievement of teachers' practices of parent involvement. In J. L. Epstein (Ed.), *School, family, and community partnerships: Preparing educators and improving schools* (pp. 221–235). Westview Press.

Family Strengthening Policy Center. (2004). *Parental involvement in education.* National Human Services Assembly. https://www.aecf.org/resources/parental-involvement-in-education

Federal Communications Commission. (2024). *Affordable connectivity program.* https://www.fcc.gov/acp

Ferlazzo, L. (2011). Involvement or engagement? *Educational Leadership, 68*(8).

Fisher, D., & Frey, N. (2022). Community circles build restorative school cultures. *Educational Leadership, 80*(1), 74–75.

Fullan, M. (2012). *Building capacity: The key to success.* https://rryshke.org/2012/11/01/building-capacity-the-key-to-success

Furtado, K., Vargas, C., Corbett, L., & Dwight, D. (2020). *Still separate, still unequal: A call to level the uneven education playing field in St. Louis.* Forward Through Ferguson. https://stillunequal.org/funding/#:~:text=In%202018%2D19%2C%20the%20median,majority%20Black%20district%20spent%20%2421%2C917

Garcia, R. (2022). Ross elementary principal Nick Gardner has big plans to make school the best in Topeka. *The Topeka Capital-Journal.* https://www.cjonline.com/story/news/education/2022/07/17/ross-elementary-principal-nick-gardner-has-vision-east-topeka-public-schools-501/7831290001/

Hanover Research. (2020). *Research priority brief: Best practices for implementing equity walks.* https://wasa-oly.org/WASA/images/WASA/6.0%20Resources/Equity/RESEARCH%20BRIEF---EQUITY%20WALKS.pdf

Hanover Research. (2022). *Research priority brief: Best practices for implementing equity walks.* https://f.hubspotusercontent00.net/hubfs/3409306/Best-Practices-in-Implementing-Equity-Walks.pdf

Hattie, J. (2008). *Visible learning: A synthesis of over 800 meta-analyses related to achievement.* Routledge.

Henderson, A. T., & Mapp, K. L. (2002). *A new wave of evidence: The impact of school, family, and community connections on student achievement.* Southwest Educational Development Laboratory.

Henderson, A. T., & Mapp, K. L. (2016). *A new wave of evidence: The impact of school, family, and the community connections on student achievement.* SEDL. Retrieved March 3, 2016, from https://www.sedl.org/connections/resources/evidence.pdf

Henderson, A. T., Mapp, K. L., Johnson, V. R., & Davies, D. (2007). *Beyond the bake sale: The essential guide to family-school partnerships.* The New Press.

Herbert, B. (2000). *Dune: House Harkonnen.* Bantam Books.

Hill, J. (2015). *The damaging impact of self-preservation and how to reverse it.* Medium.com. https://medium.com/giant-worldwide/the-damaging-impact-of-self-preservation-and-how-to-reverse-it-b03075e39963

Hollie, S. (2017). *Culturally and linguistically responsive teaching and learning: Classroom practices for student success* (2nd ed.). Shell Education.

Hoover-Dempsey, K. V., Walker, J. M. T., & Sandler, H. M. (2005). Parents' motivations for involvement in their children's education. In E. N. Patrikakou., R. P. Weissberg., S. Redding., & H. J. Walberg (Eds.), *School-family partnerships for children's success* (pp. 1–17). Teachers College Press.

Hoover-Dempsey, K. V., Walker, J. M. T., Sandler, H. M., Whetsel, D., Green, C. L., Wilkins, A. S., & Jose, P. E. (2005). Why do parents become involved? Research findings and implications. *The Elementary School Journal, 106,* 105–130.

Hughes, W., & Pickeral, T. (2013). *School climate and shared leadership.* National School Climate Center.

HundrEd. (2023). *Parents as allies.* https://hundred.org/en/collections/parents-as-allies-2-0

Impact Avenues. (2022). *Impact avenues three-year report: 2019–2020 through 2021–2022.* https://www.topeka.org/impact-avenues/

Jackson, C. K., Johnson, R. C., & Persico, C. (2015). *The effects of school spending on educational and economic outcomes: Evidence from school finance reforms.* National Bureau of Economic Research. https://www.nber.org/papers/w20847

Johnson, T. (2022). How does educational leadership help strengthen parent and family partnerships? *Blog Post.* https://www.graduateprogram.org/2022/11/how-does-educational-leadership-help-strengthen-parent-and-family-partnerships/

Kennedy, L. (2019). 6 actionable ways to use school funding more efficiently. *Prodigy Blog.* https://www.prodigygame.com/main-en/blog/school-funding/#6-ways

Klevan, S., Daniel, J., Fehrer, K., & Maier, A. (2023). *Creating the conditions for children to learn: Oakland's districtwide community schools initiative.* Learning Policy Institute. https://learningpolicyinstitute.org/media/4041/download?inline&file=OUSD_Case_Study_REPORT.pdf

Krashen, S., Lee, S., & McQuillan, J. (2012). Is the library important? Multivariate studies at the national and international level. *Journal of Language and Literacy Education, 8*(1), 26–36.

Krijnen, E., van Steensel, R., Meeuwisse, M., & Severiens, S. (2022). Aiming for educational partnership between parents and professionals: Shared vision development in a professional learning community. *School Community Journal, 32*(1), 265–300.

Landers, A. (1975). *The Dispatch.* October 4, 1975. https://news.google.com/newspapers?id=io0bAAAAIBAJ&sjid=dVEEAAAAIBAJ&dq=if-you-think-education-is-expensive-try-ignorance&pg=7016%2C3135108

Leo, A., Wilcox, K. C., & Lawson, H. (2019). Culturally response and asset-based strategies for family engagement in odds-beating secondary schools. *School Community Journal, 29*(2), 255–280.

Lewis, L. L., Kim, Y. A., & Bey, J. A. (2011). Teaching practices and strategies to involve inner-city parents at home and in the school. *Teaching and Teacher Education, 27*(1), 221–234.

Library of Congress. *Every Student Succeeds Act of 2015 (ESSA).* (2015). https://www.congress.gov/114/plaws/publ95/PLAW-114publ95.pdf

Lieberman, M. (2023). Letting students decide where money should go: How one district did it. *EdWeek.*

Lindsay, J. (2010). *Children's access to print material and education-related outcomes: Findings from a meta-analytic review.* Learning Point Associates.

Lloyd, T. (2016). *Why did the superintendent cross the road? To save money for her schools.* All Things Considered National Public Radio segment. Transcript accessed at: https://www.npr.org/transcripts/474166198

Mapp, K., & Bergman, E. (2021). *Embracing a new normal: Toward a more liberatory approach to family engagement.* Carnegie Corporation of New York.

Martin, A. (2022). *Massachusetts public schools among best in nation, according to new study.* Boston University News Service.

Maxwell, J. C. (2014). *Quotes from John Maxwell: Insights on leadership.* B&H Publishing Group.

McKillip, M., & Luhm, T. (2020). *Investing additional resources in schools serving low-income students: Evidence for advocates.* Educational Law Center. https://files.eric.ed.gov/fulltext/ED609061.pdf

Minkin, R., & Horowitz, J. M. (2023). *Parenting in America.* Pew Research Center. https://www.pewresearch.org/social-trends/2023/01/24/parenting-in-america-today/

Murphy, J. (2010). *The educator's handbook for understanding and closing the achievement gap.* Corwin.

Murphy, J., & Tobin, K. (2011). *Homelessness comes to school.* Corwin.

National Alliance on Mental Illness (NAMI). (2014). *Parents as teachers and allies program.* https://www.namica.org/webdocs/program_documents/fliers/PTasA_Talking_Points_Jan2014.pdf

National Alliance to End Homelessness. (2023). *State of homelessness 2023 edition.* https://endhomelessness.org/homelessness-in-america/homelessness-statistics/state-of-homelessness/#homelessness-in-2022

National Center for Education Statistics (NCES). (2022). *Back-to-school statistics.* https://nces.ed.gov/fastfacts/display.asp?id=372#PK12-enrollment

National Endowment for Financial Education. (2016). *Perspectives on evaluation in financial education: Landscape, issues, and studies.* https://toolkit.nefe.org/evaluation-resources/evaluation-perspectives/financial-education-groups/low-income-consumers

Nero, M. (2019). Capistrano unified could save millions, thanks to solar panels. *Patch.* https://patch.com/california/sanjuancapistrano/capistrano-unified-could-save-millions-thanks-solar-panels

Neuman, S., & Celano, D. (2001). Access to print in low-income and middle-income communities: An ecological study of four neighborhoods. *Reading Research Quarterly, 36,* 8–26.

Obama, B. (2008). *Barack Obama's Feb. 5 speech.* https://www.nytimes.com/2008/02/05/us/politics/05text-obama.html

Parents as Teachers. (2024). *Home page.* https://parentsasteachers.org/origin-story/

Rowe, A. (2018). *Digital library cards are offering thousands of ebooks to everyone.* https://www.forbes.com/sites/adamrowe1/2018/11/26/digital-library-cards-are-offering-thousands-of-ebooks-to-everyone/?sh=3772144a68f6

Rubin, A. (2023). *Massive school dissatisfaction gaps pits parents against everyone else.* https://www.axios.com/2023/08/31/us-school-education-satisfaction-survey-2023

Ruelle, P. (2019). Lessons in learning: Study shows students in 'active learning' classrooms learn more than they think. *Harvard Gazette.* https://news.harvard.edu/gazette/story/2019/09/study-shows-that-students-learn-more-when-taking-part-in-classrooms-that-employ-active-learning-strategies/

School-Based Health Alliance. (2022). *Findings from the 2022 national census of school-based health centers.* https://sbh4all.org/wp-content/uploads/2023/10/FINDINGS-FROM-THE-2022-NATIONAL-CENSUS-OF-SCHOOL-BASED-HEALTH-CENTERS-09.20.23.pdf

Simington, J. (2015). *Make schools the center of the community.* Urban Institute. https://www.urban.org/urban-wire/make-schools-center-community

Simon, S. (2001). Cries unanswered, Dog Mauls Boy. *Los Angeles Times.* https://www.latimes.com/archives/la-xpm-2001-mar-09-mn-35446-story.html

Stanford, L. (2023). Does parental involvement really help students? Here's what the research says. *EdWeek.* https://www.edweek.org/leadership/does-parent-involvement-really-help-students-heres-what-the-research-says/2023/07

The Policy Circle. (2023). *Education K–12.* Policy Brief. https://www.thepolicycircle.org/brief/k-12-education-reform/

Thoreau, H. D. (1851). *Journal 5 August 1851.* https://www.oxfordreference.com/display/10.1093/acref/9780191843730.001.0001/q-oro-ed5-00010905

Torre, D., & Murphy, J. (2016). Communities of parental engagement: New foundations for school leaders' work. *International Journal of Leadership in Education, 19*(2), 203–223.

Tschannen-Moran, M., & Barr, M. (2004). Fostering student learning: The relationship of collective teacher efficacy and student achievement. *Leadership and Policy in Schools, 3*(3), 189–209.

US Bureau of Labor and Statistics. (2023). *A profile of the working poor, 2021.* https://www.bls.gov/opub/reports/working-poor/2021/home.htm

US Department of Energy. (2002). *Myths about energy in schools.* National Renewable Energy Laboratory. https://www.nrel.gov/docs/fy02osti/31607.pdf

US Department of Health and Human Services. (2017). *School health index: A self-assessment and planning guide.* Elementary School Version. Centers for Disease Control and Prevention.

US Department of Health and Human Services. (2024). *Healthy people 2030: Social determinants of health.* Office of Disease Prevention and Health Promotion. Retrieved February 2, 2024, from https://health.gov/healthypeople/priority-areas/social-determinants-health

US Department of Agriculture. (2022). *Food security in the US: Key statistics and graphics.* https://www.ers.usda.gov/topics/food-nutrition-assistance/food-security-in-the-u-s/key-statistics-graphics/#foodsecure

Upward Bound Wichita Prep. (2024). *Homepage.* https://www.wichita.edu/services/diversity/TRIO/upward_bound_wichita_prep/

USA Facts. (2020). *Internet access.* https://usafacts.org/articles/internet-access-students-at-home/

Walsh, B. (2015). *Parent-teacher partnership: Four trends reshaping the traditional parent-teacher conference.* Harvard Graduate School of Education. https://www.gse.harvard.edu/ideas/usable-knowledge/15/10/parent-teacher-partnership

Warren, M. R., Hong, S., Rubin, C. L., & Sychitkokhong, P. U. (2009). Beyond the bake sale: A community-based relational approach to parent engagement in schools. *Teachers College Record, 111*(9), 2209–2254.

Wiggins, G., & McTighe, J. (2005). *Understanding by design* (expanded 2nd ed.). ASCD.

Wilde, M. (2023). *The ins and outs of school finance.* Greatschools.org. https://www.greatschools.org/gk/articles/the-ins-and-outs-of-school-finance/

Xiao, J. J. (Ed.). (2016). *Handbook of consumer finance research* (2nd ed.). Springer Cham. https://doi.org/10.1007/978-3-319-28887-1

Index

A Sage Company

Helping educators make the greatest impact

CORWIN HAS ONE MISSION: to enhance education through intentional professional learning.

We build long-term relationships with our authors, educators, clients, and associations who partner with us to develop and continuously improve the best evidence-based practices that establish and support lifelong learning.